Thanksgiving Psalms
A Path to Praise

Discovery Guide

Jerome and Sandra Boone

All Scripture quotations, unless otherwise indicated,
are taken from the *New King James Version*® (NKJV).
Copyright © 1979, 1980, 1982, 1990, 1995, Thomas Nelson Inc., Publishers.
Used by permission.

Scripture quotations marked NASB
are from the *New American Standard Bible* ®.
Copyright © 1960, 1963, 1968, 1971, 1972, 1973, 1975, 1977, 1995
by The Lockman Foundation. Used by permission.

Scripture quotations marked KJV
are taken from The Holy Bible, *King James Version*. (public domain)

Scripture quotations marked MEV
are taken from *The Holy Bible, Modern English Version*.
Copyright © 2014 by Military Bible Association.
Published and distributed by Charisma House.
Used by permission.

Scripture quotations marked NIV
are taken from *The Holy Bible, New International Version®*, NIV®.
Copyright © 1973, 1978, 1984, 2011 by Biblica, Inc.®
Used by permission. All rights reserved worldwide. www.zondervan.com

Scripture taken from *The Message*.
Copyright © 1993, 1994, 1995, 1996, 2000, 2001, 2002.
Used by permission of NavPress Publishing Group.

Scripture quotations taken from the *Amplified® Bible* (AMP),
Copyright © 2015 by The Lockman Foundation
Used by permission. www.Lockman.org

ISBN: 978-1-940682-47-1
Copyright® 2016, Church of God Adult Discipleship,
Cleveland, Tennessee
All Rights Reserved. No portion of this book may be reproduced
in any form without written permission from Church of God Adult Discipleship.
Printed in the United States of America

TABLE OF CONTENTS

THANKSGIVING PRAISE
PREFACE 7

INDUCTIVE BIBLE STUDY
INTRODUCTORY SESSION ...... INTRODUCTION TO INDUCTIVE STUDY OF THANKSGIVING PSALMS 11

PSALMS: THE BOOK OF PRAISE
LESSON ONE 29

PRAISE AS THANKSGIVING
LESSON TWO 45

PRAISE IS THE RIGHTFUL RESPONSE TO GOD'S HELP
LESSON THREE .... PSALM 30 61

GOD'S STRENGTH BRINGS JOY AND PRAISE
LESSON FOUR ...... PSALM 21 87

GOD'S FORGIVENESS IS JOY FOREVERMORE
LESSON FIVE .... PSALM 32 115

TASTE AND SEE THAT THE LORD IS GOOD
LESSON SIX .... PSALM 34 141

IT IS GOOD TO GIVE THANKS TO THE LORD

    Lesson Seven..... Psalm 92 169

PRAISE GOD, HIS MERCY ENDURES FOREVER

    Lesson Eight..... Psalm 118 199

PRAISE GOD WITH YOUR WHOLE HEART

    Lesson Nine....... Psalm 138 231

PRAISE GOD, HE DELIVERS FROM DISTRESS

    Lesson Ten .... Psalm 107 263

PRAISE GOD, OUR HELP IN TIMES OF NEED

    Lesson Eleven .. Psalm 124 287

PRAISE GOD, HE DELIVERS FROM DEATH

    Lesson Twelve.. Jonah 2 311

ABOUT THE AUTHOR 337

PREFACE

Praising God is the highest priority for both the church and the Christian. It will continue to be the activity of God's people when His kingdom has fully come. Praise is the vital, eternal connection between God and His people, and the Book of Psalms plays a key role in this relationship. The people of Israel treasured Psalms as their worship hymnal. The early church embraced Psalms as a fitting expression of praise to the triune God: Father, Son, and Holy Spirit. For Christians today, the Book of Psalms is a path to praise.

Thanksgiving psalms, in particular, focus on praising God for His lovingkindness. They express gratitude for what God has done. This Bible study will enable you to better understand worshipful praise—the kind of praise that glorifies God. Lesson One introduces you to the book of Psalms as part of inspired Scripture. Lesson Two acquaints you with different styles of thanksgiving psalms. Lessons Three through Nine cover psalms of thanksgiving, originally offered by individual Israelites, such as King David, while Lessons Ten and Eleven consider thanksgiving psalms used by the Old Testament community of faith. Lesson Twelve explores a Thanksgiving psalm located outside the Book of Psalms and its historical context.

After your study of the thanksgiving psalms, you will have a greater appreciation for biblical praise. Look for opportunities to incorporate what you learn in your private devotions and church services. The process of inductive Bible study sharpens biblical interpretation skills and allows for engagement with the Holy Spirit. We pray that this Bible study will inspire you to declare with the psalmist, "The LORD is my strength and my shield; My heart trusted in Him, and I am helped; Therefore my heart greatly rejoices, And with my song I will praise Him" (Psalm 28:7).

Jerome & Sandra Boone

Introductory Session

Thanksgiving

A Path to Praise

Introduction to Inductive Study Of Thanksgiving Psalms

INTRODUCTION SESSION

INTRODUCTION TO INDUCTIVE STUDY OF THANKSGIVING PSALMS

Key Verse

Let everything that has breath praise the LORD. Praise the LORD! (Psalm 150:6).

Welcome

Hallelujah! The universal word of praise. God's people in every country and of every language recognize the word. It simply means "praise God." In addition to expressing praise to God, it identifies the speaker as one of God's people. The powerful word, hallelujah, is the very keynote of the Book of Psalms. Just as we testify to God's goodness and sing praises in worship, the people of God celebrated His lovingkindness in songs of praise thousands of years ago. Consequently, the Book of Psalms has been as universally used and timelessly enjoyed as the very theme upon which it is built.

INTRODUCTORY SESSION

The Psalms are made up of five books, which include four categories: Psalms of Lamentation, Wisdom, Thanksgiving and Hymns. You are about to embark upon an inductive study of the Thanksgiving Psalms. These psalms project the celebration of deliverance and reflect the joy of release through praise. As you dig into this treasure trove of Scripture, it is our hope that you will experience this joy through discovery and application.

During this study, you will be using the inductive Bible study method. This INTRODUCTORY SESSION is an explanation of this enjoyable way of exploring God's Word. If inductive Bible study is new to you, please read the material carefully. If you have done another *Enliven Encountering God through His Word* study, you will be familiar with this method of exploring God's Word. If so, you may want to simply skim this material to refresh your memory before moving on to your study of the Thanksgiving Psalms.

A Review of Inductive Bible Study

During your study of *Thanksgiving Psalms*, a great treasure of truth is waiting in the Word of God for your discovery and spiritual benefit. A solid way of uncovering this truth and being transformed by it is the inductive study of God's Word. This approach to the study of the Scriptures begins with the Bible itself and requires that you follow the steps listed below.

The Four Steps

During your inductive Bible study of *Thanksgiving Psalms*, in order for you to receive maximum

Introduction to Inductive Study for Thanksgiving Psalms

benefit in each lesson, you will begin by reading some introductory remarks to the passage of Scripture that you will be studying. You will then participate in four basic steps:

1. **DISCOVER** (*observation*)
2. **DISCERN** (*interpretation*)
3. **DEVOTE** (*reflection & prayer*)
4. **DISCIPLE** (*application*)

Pause for Prayer

As you move through your study, you will be invited to *Pause for Prayer* and to become present with God during your study time. Bible study best takes place in an atmosphere of prayer, in conversation with God. The Holy Spirit has inspired the Word of God. What has been given by the Spirit is to be interpreted by the aid of the Spirit. Prayer opens our hearts to the Holy Spirit and allows Him to guide us in the learning process. Communication with and receptiveness to the Spirit bring forth truth from God's Word that stimulates discipleship and spiritual growth.

As you Pause for Prayer during your study time, there are various ways that you might choose to pray. In addition to inviting the Holy Spirit's presence into your time of study, you might thank God for His truths and blessings that you are receiving through His Word, or ask Him to move in a specific way in your life or in the world. During these moments of prayer, it can be helpful to focus on

INTRODUCTORY SESSION

a particular passage from God's Word in a reflective, prayerful way. In this *Discovery Guide*, during your Pause for Prayer, you will be given an opportunity to reflect on and pray about passages from Psalms.

STEP 1-DISCOVER

Observation: Observe & Uncover the Facts • Using *Helping Questions*

Asking: "What do I see in this passage?"

Each week following your reading of the introductory remarks in your *Discovery Guide* about the passage, the first step you will take in your own inductive Bible study of Thanksgiving Psalms will be to read and focus on the content of a portion of Scripture. This initial reading is best done carefully and prayerfully.

Using Helping Questions

To help you begin to **DISCOVER** (uncover and observe) the wonderful truths of God's Word, you will be asked to formulate questions that will help you notice and see the facts and truths in that particular passage of Scripture. In each lesson, you will be given the opportunity to create Helping Questions (asking Who? What? When? Where? Why? How?) in order to help you explore the biblical text.

Introduction to Inductive Study for Thanksgiving Psalms

As you begin to ask Helping Questions, be open to the Holy Spirit and what the writer is saying. You might want to make notes about any meanings that begin to emerge, so that you can explore them further when it is time to interpret and **DISCERN** the meaning of the text.

Each week during this **DISCOVER** point of your study, in addition to reading the biblical text and introductory remarks for the lesson and creating Helping Questions, you may also want to quickly review LESSON ONE and LESSON TWO.

STEP 2-DISCERN

Interpretation: **Interpret & Understand the Meaning • Using Helping Tools**

Asking: **"What is the meaning of this passage?"**

The Holy Spirit is our great teacher. He works together with us to illuminate our understanding, as we are steadfast in our study of God's Word. You remember Paul's words in 2 Timothy 2:15: "Study to show yourself approved by God, a workman who need not be ashamed, rightly dividing the word of truth" (MEV). Worthwhile Bible study involves real study and requires diligence on our part. There are great treasures to be *discovered* and *discerned* by studying the Word. In each lesson, we will ask for the Holy Spirit's help as we begin to *discern* (*interpret*) the truths in a particular passage of God's Word.

16 Introductory Session

Using Helping Tools

During this second **DISCERN** step of your study, you will have the opportunity to mark important words and phrases. Using colored pencils or highlighters, you will get to be creative and have fun underlining, circling, highlighting, or marking in some way phrases and verses. These markings that you apply will be your Helping Tools that will assist you in discerning the meaning of the passage.

As you mark the text, you will begin to notice some key terms and concepts, and will also see some patterns and repetitions emerging in Paul's discussion. Use whatever markings work best for you. This step is meant to be a fun one that helps you personally. Some examples of Helping Tools that you might create are:

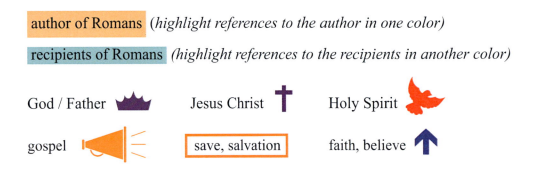

Discerning What the Bible Says

Once you have marked the text with your Helping Tools, you will begin to explore the meaning

Introduction to Inductive Study for Thanksgiving Psalms

of the passage by looking for the meaning in the Bible itself. In inductive Bible study, the meaning of a passage is always to be explored in the Bible first, in light of the passage's context within the book of the Bible of which it is a part.

As you look over the passage that you have marked with Helping Tools, carefully think about the words and reflect on them. Should you struggle with the interpretation (the meaning), you may want to refer to some Bible study aids such as a commentary, Bible dictionary, word study, or other theological work. (For a list of additional print and online resources, see "Helpful Supplies & Resources" on page 23 of this *Discovery Guide*.)

Using Various Bible Versions

The Protestant principle is that each person is to be encouraged to read the Bible in his or her own language. The scriptural quotations of this publication, unless otherwise noted, are from the *New King James Version* (NKJV). Along with using the NKJV, comparison of different translations can be very helpful for gaining a fuller understanding of the passage you are studying. BibleGateway.com and BibleStudyTools.com are good online resources for Bible version comparison.

STEP 3-DEVOTE

Reflection & Prayer: **Reflect, Pray & Be Transformed • Through Conversation with God & Journaling**

Asking: *"God, what do You want to say to me through your Word?"*

We study God's Word to be changed and to be strengthened, not merely to accumulate information. That is why you are studying to understand a passage of Scripture—so that you can experience the transforming power of truth.

Once you have completed the **DISCOVER** and **DISCERN** steps, it is important to take some time to reflect and pray about what you have learned and experienced during your time of study. God wants to speak to you and bless you. This **DEVOTE** (*reflection and prayer*) step of inductive Bible study is a wonderful opportunity for you to experience God in a fresh, new way. During this time, you may *devote* (dedicate) yourself to God and His call by reflecting on His Word, receiving instruction from Him, and allowing His Spirit to change, bless, and equip you.

A good way to begin this special devotion time with God is to sit quietly in His presence for a few moments, inviting Him to quiet your mind and to help you focus on Him. In each lesson, you will be given an opportunity to prepare your heart through a Pause for Prayer, in which you will be invited to reflect on a verse of Scripture.

Introduction to Inductive Study for Thanksgiving Psalms

Following your reflection on God's Word, you will then encounter in your *Discovery Guide* a few reflection questions for that particular lesson that will help you open your heart to God and ask Him how He wants to use this passage of Scripture to transform you.

In addition to considering these reflection questions, you may also want to look through any notes that you have made in your journal or *Discovery Guide*, to help you identify how God wants to move in your heart and life.

Some possible questions that you might want to ask God during this **DEVOTE** step of your inductive Bible study are:

- ☐ God, who are You calling me to be—How do You want to change and transform me?
- ☐ Do You want to clarify any misperceptions that I might have had in the past?
- ☐ Are You calling me to repentance and change in any areas of my life?
- ☐ How do You want me to grow, especially in faith and trust in You?
- ☐ In what ways are You calling me to a deeper level of commitment to You and Your Word?
- ☐ What would You have me do in light of what I have learned?
- ☐ Are You calling me to some new aspect of service or ministry?

Remember, this is time for a very personal conversation with God during which He wants to bless you. As you receive knowledge, healing, inspiration, direction, or inclinations of calling, be sure to note those in your notebook or journal. This way you will have them to return to later for remembering, further exploration, prayer, or action.

STEP 4-DISCIPLE

Application: Apply & Live God's Word • Through Commitment & Action

Asking: (1) "What is the meaning for today—in my life and in the world?"

(2) "How can and will I act on what I have learned?"

The next natural step following your **DEVOTE** time with God is for you to begin to live what you have learned—to be a disciple. This will involve your taking what you have experienced with God during this study and putting it into action—in your own life, within your relationship with others, and out in the larger world.

In this **DISCIPLE** step of inductive Bible study, you will have an opportunity to ask God through His Holy Spirit to direct you and give you wisdom regarding what actions He is calling you to take. God promises that He will help each of us in this process. Through the power of His Spirit, we can grow and make changes in our lives, and develop new habits and ways of being and doing things. We can also learn how to share our personal experiences of God's saving love with others in ways that

Introduction to Inductive Study for Thanksgiving Psalms

are unique to us, using the gifts and talents God has given us. We can learn to be disciples and make disciples (Matt. 28:19).

As you think about how the passage of Scripture you are studying applies to the church and the world today, ask God how you might move forward in living out the truths of His Word. Consider if you want to make any commitments or make any plans to do so. You might note any thoughts, inspirations, creative ideas, commitments, plans, or questions in your notebook or journal, so that you have them for future reference for action, prayer, or sharing with others.

Instructions for Using Your Discovery Guide

As part of each lesson, you will begin by reading the Key Verse and an Introduction to the passage of Scripture you will be studying. You will then be invited to Pause for Prayer, following which you will read the actual text of the passage of Scripture. Once you have completed your reading, you will begin to move through your inductive Bible study steps: **DISCOVER, DISCERN, DEVOTE,** and **DISCIPLE.**

Along the way, while moving through your *Discovery Guide*, you will be invited to interact with the text in various ways. You may be asked to complete a sentence, list your ideas, answer questions, rewrite a scriptural thought in your own words, compare the Scripture with other passages, identify a core focus and other major themes (topics) of the passage, or to do other similar activities. Please take each exercise seriously. Think about what you are being asked to do. After you have written your answer, read it carefully and prayerfully. You may want to revise it and rewrite it, as you gain more insight. What you write is for your own benefit; it will not be judged or read by anyone else. In group sessions, you will be asked to share only what you are comfortable sharing.

Inductive Bible study allows you to teach yourself. If you are a part of a class or a group that is doing this study, you will likely have the opportunity to share from time to time some of your thoughts, feelings, or insights with others in your group. As a member of a class or study group, it is very important that you do the exercises of the assigned lesson before you meet each time, so that you are prepared to gain from and contribute to the group's time together.

Partnering with the Holy Spirit

Vital to your discipleship is becoming a partner with the Holy Spirit and relying on Him in Christian living and service. As you explore Psalms, we pray that you will feel the Holy Spirit's presence and love. May you be empowered by Him and learn to follow His promptings in all areas of life—and through your study, devotions, and public worship, become more like Christ each day.

Helpful Supplies & Resources

ESSENTIAL

- ☐ Bible—(NKJV is primarily used in this study).
- ☐ Colored pens or pencils, highlighters
- ☐ Notebook or journal

RECOMMENDED

- ☐ How to do inductive Bible study—*Enliven Encountering God Through His Word* Bible study. William A. Simmons. Church of God Adult Discipleship, 2014.

- ☐ A study Bible—such as *Fire Bible* (NIV 1984, KJV, or ESV), Hendrickson Publishers. *Fire Bible* (MEV), Passio. (Former titles: *Full Life Study Bible* and *Life in the Spirit Study Bible*).

ONLINE

- ☐ *BibleGateway.com* www.biblegateway.com
  Offers various Bible versions and study tools.

- ☐ *BibleStudyTools.com* www.biblestudytools.com

  Offers various Bible versions and study tools, including a helpful word study resource <u>Strong's Exhaustive Concordance</u> (linked from KJV and NASB to Hebrew and Greek lexicons).

- ☐ Audio Bible—www.biblegateway.com/resources/audio/, www.biblestudytools.com/audio-bible/, www.bible.is/download/audio

- ☐ Additional online tools, such as:

Biblia.com, BlueLetterBible.org, and StudyLight.org.

OPTIONAL

Your local public or church library may have the following types of resources in their reference or circulating collections:

- ☐ Bible handbook—such as: *Halley's Bible Handbook*. Henry H. Halley. Zondervan, 2014.

- ☐ Bible commentary—one-volume or a multi-volume set, such as *Zondervan Illustrated Bible Backgrounds Commentary*. Clinton E. Arnold. Zondervan, 2002.

- ☐ Bible dictionary, encyclopedia, or concordance, such as:

Evangelical Dictionary of Biblical Theology. Walter A. Elwell. Baker Books, 2001. 1996 edition: http://www.biblestudytools.com/dictionaries/.

Strong's Exhaustive Concordance—
   The New Strong's Expanded Exhaustive Concordance of the Bible. James Strong. Thomas Nelson, 2010. Online: www.biblestudytools.com (Search a single verse in KJV or NASB, and select "Interlinear" to view the concordance linked to Hebrew and Greek lexicons.)

Vine's Complete Expository Dictionary of Old and New Testament Words. W. E. Vine, Merrill F. Unger, William White, Jr. Thomas Nelson, 1996.

A Closing Prayer of Blessing

Grace and peace be yours in abundance through the knowledge of God and of Jesus our Lord. His divine power has given us everything we need for a godly life through our knowledge of him who called us by his own glory and goodness (2 Peter 1:2-4, NIV).

Lesson One

Thanksgiving

A Path to Praise

Psalms: The Book of Praise

LESSON ONE
PSALMS: THE BOOK OF PRAISE
OVERVIEW

Praise the LORD!
Praise God in His sanctuary;
Praise Him in His mighty expanse.
Praise Him for His mighty deeds;
Praise Him according to His excellent greatness.
Praise Him with trumpet sound;
Praise Him with harp and lyre.
Praise Him with timbrel and dancing;
Praise Him with stringed instruments and pipe.
Praise Him with loud cymbals;
Praise Him with resounding cymbals.
Let everything that has breath praise the LORD.
Praise the LORD! (Psalm 150, NASB)

Although Psalm 150 is the closing doxology (or expression of praise) in the Book of Psalms, it serves as a fitting introduction to our study. The entire Book of Psalms echoes the same theme as Psalm 150: Praise the Lord!

The place to begin any study of a biblical book is with its origin, purpose, and structure. Who wrote it? Why? How do the chapters fit together? These questions and others will be answered in this lesson. We will consider the name and nature of the psalms, the authors of the psalms, the structure of the psalms, and the titles of individual psalms.

Learning Objectives

After completing this lesson, you should be able to:

1. Discuss the origin and meaning of the title Psalms.

2. Name and describe four major types of psalms.

3. Relate the evidence for multiple authorship of the Book of Psalms and name as many as seven of its authors.

4. State the number of psalms in the Book of Psalms and the number of volumes into which it is divided.

5. Define the word doxology and discuss its relationship to the structure of Psalms.

6. Explain the importance of the psalm titles and their relationships to the original psalms.

PSALMS: THE BOOK OF PRAISE

The Name and Nature of the Psalms

The English title Psalms refers to songs accompanied by musical instruments and comes from the Greek translation of the Old Testament, the Septuagint (LXX). Psalms is an appropriate title in our English Bibles since that is exactly how the New Testament refers to the book (see Luke 20:42; 24:44; Acts 1:20; 13:33). The Hebrew Bible appropriately refers to the book as Hymns.

As other hymnals intended for public worship, the book of Psalms contains a variety of themes. Some psalms are glad while others are sad. Some extol godly wisdom while others cry out for forgiveness. Many psalms have multiple themes. Any attempt to divide the psalms into neat categories will be difficult, but it is worthwhile to organize the psalms into categories for purpose of this study.

The Book of Psalms is very different in style compared to the New Testament gospels and epistles. It does not develop a single theme or present an organized discussion. Instead, it is a collection of songs from many generations of Israel's history. Consequently, the best way to study the psalms is to organize them around common themes and study them group by group.

There are two basic approaches to categorizing the psalms. The more traditional method focuses on content, while the more popular method concentrates on function. Modern commentaries on the Book of Psalms typically categorize by function and that method will be used in this study. The Book of Psalms consists of psalms of lamentation, wisdom, thanksgiving, and hymns. The following descriptions will aid our understanding of the psalms:

- **Lamentation Psalms:** These psalms record the cries of people in distress resulting from personal tragedy or national crisis.

- **Wisdom Psalms:** These psalms emphasize godly wisdom and teach the importance of righteousness.

- **Thanksgiving Psalms:** These psalms express praise in response to the Lord's help.

- **Hymns**: These psalms glorify God's lovingkindness and faithfulness in a more general way than the thanksgiving psalms.

BIBLE ASSIGNMENT

Read an example of each psalm category in your Bible.

1. *Lamentation:* Psalm 13
2. *Wisdom:* Psalm 37
3. *Thanksgiving:* Psalm 107
4. *Hymn:* Psalm 100

The Authors of the Psalms

The Book of Psalms differs significantly from the New Testament books in the matter of authorship. Rather than being the product of a single author, the Book of Psalms contains the works of many authors. Although many Christians associate the Book of Psalms with David, the psalms contain positive proof of many authors.

Psalms: The Book of Praise

The grouping of the psalms confirms the book's multiple authorship. For instance, Psalms 42-49 are "of the sons of Korah" while Psalms 73-83 are "of Asaph." Other groupings emerge as you read the titles of the individual psalms.

At least seven authors contributed to the book: Moses, David, Solomon, the Sons of Korah, Asaph, Ethan, and Heman.

- Moses delivered the Hebrews out of Egyptian bondage and played an integral role in bringing the Ten Commandments to Israel. He wrote Psalm 90.

- David lived as a man after God's own heart. As king, he organized the religion of Israel and made Jerusalem its capital. He wrote Psalms 3-9, 11-32, 34-41, 51-65, 68-70, 86, 101, 103, 108-110, 122, 124, 131, 133, 138-145.

- Solomon, David's son, became known throughout the ancient Near East for his wisdom. He wrote many proverbs and psalms, including Psalms 72 and 127.

- The Sons of Korah descended from the tribe of Levi and served as singers in the temple service (2 Chronicles 20:19). The Sons of Korah wrote Psalms 42, 44-49, 84-85, 87-88.

- Asaph descended from the family of Gershom of the tribe of Levi. He served as a musician during the reign of David and the temple under Solomon. Scripture refers to him as a prophet (2 Chronicles 29:30). He wrote Psalms 50, 73-83.

- Ethan descended from the family of Merari of the tribe of Levi. David appointed him as a music leader for Israel and he was known for his wisdom (1 Kings 4:31). He wrote Psalm 89.

- Heman was one of the Sons of Korah. David appointed him as a music leader for Israel. He ~~is~~ wrote Psalm 88.

Although conclusive proof exists of the multiple authorship of the psalms, we have good reason to think of David when we think of Psalms. David contributed more to the Book of Psalms than any other author. Of the 150 psalms, David wrote 73 and probably started the collection of songs which we know as the Book of Psalms. Scholars believe David began compiling the Book of Psalms in about 1000 B.C. and it was completed near the end of the Old Testament period (about 500-400 B.C.).

BIBLE ASSIGNMENT

What can we learn about David and his gift and ministry of music in these Scriptures?

1. 1 Samuel 16:17-18 — "Can play well" ... "the Lord is with him"
2. 2 Samuel 6:1-19 — "played instruments" ... "Danced before the Lord"
3. 1 Chronicles 16:1-43 — "played instruments" ... "Wrote songs of praise to God"

The Structure of the Psalms

The Book of Psalms consists of five volumes. Each volume concludes with a doxology.

- Book One: Psalms 1-41 – Doxology 41:13
- Book Two: Psalms 42-72 – Doxology 72:18-19
- Book Three: Psalms 73-89 – Doxology 89:52
- Book Four: Psalms 90-106 – Doxology 106:48
- Book Five: Psalms 106-150 – Doxology 150:1-6

Psalms: The Book of Praise

No one knows how the Book of Psalms came to be divided into five volumes. The book's compilers probably made the divisions to more easily locate specific psalms. In ancient days, the psalms were not numbered as they are in our Bible. Readers identified psalms by the first words of the beginning line, and it was helpful to know the section of scroll in which a psalm was found.

The specific number of volumes in the Book of Psalms results from Jewish tradition. The Pentateuch, or Torah as the Jews call it, consisted of the first five books of the Bible. The Book of Psalms was likely fashioned after its pattern.

BIBLE ASSIGNMENT

1. Identify the beginning of each volume of the Book of Psalms in your Bible. Most Bibles have the sections clearly marked with bold print.
2. Read the doxologies in order to see how each volume concludes. Notice that Psalm serves as a doxology to close the Book of Psalms.

The Titles of Individual Psalms

Of the 150 psalms, 116 include titles. Most scholars agree that the titles did not appear in the original psalms. As a result, the titles are not considered to be divinely inspired. However, they represent the earliest traditions about the psalms and should be respected.

The first titled psalm is Psalm 3. Does your Bible translation give an additional title to Psalm 3? It is important for you to recognize the difference between the psalm titles being discussed in this section and other titles that may have been added by editors in your translation. In the *New American Standard Bible*, Psalm 3 has two titles. The first, "Morning Prayer of Trust in God," is an editorial title. The translator added this title to the psalm. Because it does not appear in the Hebrew text of Psalms, we will not concern ourselves with it in this study.

The second title, "A Psalm of David, when he fled from Absalom his son," contributes to our study. This title, while probably not original with the psalm, does appear in the Hebrew text of Psalms. This title, and 115 other titles similar to it, contain details about the psalm's author, historical occasion, type, or function in worship, and musical accompaniment. Such information adds to our understanding of the full context of the psalm.

As noted in the first section of this lesson, 101 psalms include statements about authorship in their titles. Of these, David wrote 73, Asaph wrote 12, the Sons of Korah wrote 11, Solomon wrote two, and Moses, Heman, and Ethan wrote one apiece. Knowing the author of each psalm greatly helps us interpret it, just as knowing about the songwriter often deepens our appreciation of a song.

Psalm titles sometimes tell us a psalm's historical occasion or the circumstances in the psalmists life which caused him to write the psalm. Knowing the historical occasion helps the interpreter understand the mood of the psalm and illuminates the figures of speech used in the poem. Thirteen of David's psalms reveal historical occasions in their titles:

1. Psalm 3—"A Psalm of David, when he fled from Absalom his son" (see 2 Samuel 15:1-18:33).

2. Psalm 7—"A Shiggaion of David, which he sang to the Lord concerning Cush, a Benjamite."

3. Psalm 18—"A Psalm of David the servant of the Lord, who spoke to the Lord the words of this song in the day that the Lord delivered him from the hand of all his enemies and from the hand of Saul" (see 2 Samuel 22).

4. Psalm 34—"A Psalm of David when he feigned madness before Abimelech, who drove him away and he departed" (see 1 Samuel 21:13).

5. Psalm 51—"A Psalm of David, when Nathan the prophet came to him, after he had gone in to Bathsheba" (see 2 Samuel 11, 12:23).

6. Psalm 52—"A Maskil of David, when Doeg the Edomite came and told Saul and said to him, 'David has come to the house of Ahimelech'" (see 1 Samuel 22:9).

7. Psalm 54—"A Maskil of David, when the Ziphites came and said to Saul, "Is not David hiding himself among us?"'" (see 1 Samuel 23:19).

8. Psalm 56—"A Mikhtam of David, when the Philistines seized him in Gath" (see 1 Samuel 21:10-15).

9. Psalm 57—"A Mikhtam of David, when he fled from Saul in the cave" (see 1 Samuel 24:2-22).

10. Psalm 59—"A Mikhtam of David, when Saul sent men and they watched the house in order to kill him" (see 1 Samuel 19:11).

11. Psalm 60—"A Mikhtam of David, to teach; when he struggled with Aram-naharaim and with Aram-zobah, and Joab returned, and smote twelve thousand of Edom in the Valley of Salt" (see 2 Samuel 8:13).

12. Psalm 63—"A Psalm of David, when he was in the wilderness of Judah" (see 2 Samuel 15:13-30).

13. Psalm 142—"Maskil of David, when he was in the cave" (see 1 Samuel 22:1-2).

When we read the circumstances which led David to write these psalms, it's as if we are hiding in the cave with him, sensing the injustice of Saul pursuing him, or feeling his guilt of knowingly disobeying God.

BIBLE ASSIGNMENT

Read 2 Samuel 11:1-12:13 and Psalm 51. The historical occasion in 2 Samuel illuminates the meaning of Psalm 51.

Psalm titles also contain technical musical terms. Gleason L. Archer, Jr., in *A Survey of Old Testament Introduction*, defines seven types of psalms:

1. *Mizmor*—a song accompanied by instrumental music (57 psalms)
2. *Shir*—vocal music (27 psalms)
3. *Maskil*—a poem intended for meditation (13 psalms)
4. *Mikhtam*—a psalm of memorable thoughts (6 psalms)
5. *Tepillah*—a prayer (5 psalms)
6. *Shiggaion*—a wandering song (1 psalm)

These technical terms are not particularly important for our study, but they emphasize the variety of poetic material in Psalms.

Further supporting the idea of Psalms as Israel's hymnal, the psalm titles, sometimes indicate the musical tune to which the psalm was to be sung. Notice the tunes which are indicated in Psalms 9 and 22:

- Psalm 9—"*Muth-labben*" (the tune is "Death to the Son")
- Psalm 22—"*Aijeleth Hashshahar*" (the tune is "The Hind of the Morning")

At other times, the psalm titles tell which musical instruments were to accompany the psalm. The following terms occur in some titles:

1. *Alamoth*—soprano voice or high-pitched harps
2. *Neginoth*—stringed instruments
3. *Nehiloth*—perforated wind instruments, like flutes
4. *Sheminith*—eight-stringed harp (or an instruction to sing in a certain key)

Again, these technical terms do not add great value to our study, but emphasize the musical nature of the psalms, which suggests the function of the book as Israel's hymnal.

Music expresses emotion and plays a natural part in the worship of God. God's people sing when they are joyous. We can see this from the earliest pages of Scripture. God delivered Israel from Egyptian bondage and destroyed the pursuing Egyptian army in the Red Sea, and as Israel stood safely on the eastern bank, Moses celebrated the occasion with a song (Exodus 15) and Miriam accompanied him with a tambourine. Music sometimes accompanies sorrow, such as David's mourning the death of Saul and his sons as expressed in 2 Samuel 1:19-27. Psalms, a book filled with joy and sorrow, lends itself to singing.

SELF-CHECK TEST

Choose the word from the list below which best completes each following statement. (One word is used twice.)

100	hymns	Greek	Lamentations
150	author(s)	Hebrew	praises
songs	original		

1. The English title *Psalms* comes from the _Hebrew_ translation of the Old Testament.

2. The word *Psalms* refers to _songs_ accompanied by musical instruments.

3. Most scholars believe that the majority of the psalm titles were not part of the _original_ text.

4. Psalm titles are important because they contain statements about the psalms' _original_, historical occasion, type or function in worship, and musical accompaniment.

5. _Lamentation_ psalms record the cries of people in times of distress. Wisdom psalms emphasize godly wisdom. Thanksgiving psalms express praise in response to the Lord's help. _Praises_ glorify God's lovingkindness.

6. The Book of Psalms contains the works of many _authors_.

7. The Book of Psalms consists of five volumes. There are a total of _150_ psalms in the book.

Lesson Two

Thanksgiving

A Path to Praise

Praise as Thanksgiving

LESSON TWO

PRAISE AS THANKSGIVING

Give thanks to the LORD, for He is good;
For His lovingkindness is everlasting.
Oh let Israel say,
"His lovingkindness is everlasting."
Oh let the house of Aaron say,
"His lovingkindness is everlasting."
Oh let those who fear the LORD say,
"His lovingkindness is everlasting."
From my distress I called upon the LORD;
The LORD answered me and set me in a large place.
The LORD is for me; I will not fear;
What can man do to me?
The LORD is for me among those who help me;
Therefore I will look with satisfaction on those who hate me.
It is better to take refuge in the LORD

> *Than to trust in man.*
> *It is better to take refuge in the LORD*
> *Than to trust in princes.*
> *The LORD is God, and He has given us light;*
> *Bind the festival sacrifice with cords to horns of the altar.*
> *You are my God, and I give thanks to You;*
> *You are my God, I extol You.*
> *Give thanks to the LORD, for He is good;*
> *For His lovingkindness is everlasting* (Psalm 118:1-9, 27-29, NASB).

Thanksgiving psalms express the joy of release and the excitement of having been delivered out of adversity. They naturally result from experiencing the goodness of God. The psalmist essentially says, "Thank You, God, for delivering me out of trouble." Yet, thanksgiving praise is stronger, broader, and more creative than our common idea of thanks.

Thanksgiving psalms appear many times and in various styles throughout the Book of Psalms. In their simplest form, thanksgiving psalms announce the writer's intention to praise God and move immediately to expressing that praise. In the more common form, thanksgiving psalms include three distinct parts: (1) the statement of intent to praise God, (2) the report of deliverance, and (3) a concluding vow to continue praising God.

This lesson discusses thanksgiving psalms in their various styles, focusing on their three main parts. After discussing the form and component parts of thanksgiving psalms, we will cover important aspects of interpretation.

PRAISE AS THANKSGIVING

Learning Objectives

After completing this lesson you should be able to:

1. Describe the main parts of thanksgiving psalms: the introduction, main body, and conclusion.

2. Describe the nature of thanksgiving psalms.

3. Explain the presence of the renewed vow of praise in thanksgiving psalms.

_____
_____
_____
_____
_____
_____
_____
_____
_____

Learning Objectives

The opening lines of thanksgiving psalms offer clues to their purpose. Common thanksgiving psalms begin with a statement of the psalmist's intention to praise God, often expressed as "I will" or "Let us" praise God. Consider the following examples:

> *I will extol thee, O LORD; for thou hast lifted me up, and hast not made my foes to rejoice over me* (Psalm 30:1, KJV).

> *I will give You thanks with all my heart; I will sing praises to You before the gods* (Psalm 138:1, NASB).

Other thanksgiving psalm introductions include:

'I love You, O LORD, my strength.' The LORD is my rock and my fortress and my deliverer, My God, my rock, in whom I take refuge; My shield and the horn of my salvation, my stronghold (Psalm 18:1, 2 NASB).

It is good to give thanks to the LORD And to sing praises to Your name, O Most High; To declare Your lovingkindness in the morning And Your faithfulness by night, With the ten-stringed lute and with the harp, With resounding music upon the lyre (Psalm 92:1-3, NASB).

Opening lines such as these reveal the true nature of thanksgiving psalms. The psalmist's words do not merely state the facts; they are confessional in nature, testifying to God's goodness before others. The psalmist summarizes God's saving activity and calls the reader to praise.

If we could journey back to the time of the Old Testament, we could see and hear the confessional aspect of the thanksgiving psalms. If we could stand in Solomon's temple courts, we would see Israelites bring their thanksgiving offerings to the Lord (Leviticus 7:11-18). A man would come with his family and friends to present a sacrifice and burn part of it on the altar. Another portion of it would be cooked and served as part of a festival meal for the worshiper and his family and friends. At some point in the meal, the one who had offered the sacrifice to God would stand and confess why he was giving the offering. Just as we Christians use certain songs to express our praise to God, thanksgiving psalms were a common way to tell what God had done.

Lesson Two

A thanksgiving psalm's introduction may be one verse or several, but it is easy to recognize if you know its components: a statement of intent to praise God and a summary of all He has done to merit that praise.

BIBLE ASSIGNMENT

Read Psalm 116 and identify its introduction, remembering that the introductory part of the psalm has only two things:

1. A statement of intent to praise

   _____
   _____
   _____
   _____
   _____
   _____

2. A brief summary of why God is being praised

   _____
   _____
   _____
   _____
   _____
   _____

The Report of Deliverance

The report of deliverance makes up the main body of the thanksgiving psalm. In its simplest form, the report of deliverance tells about God's gracious activity in the psalmist's life. In the more common form, the report of deliverance looks back at the time of distress, remembers the cry to God for help, and tells of God's gracious deliverance.

The report of deliverance usually begins by looking back at the time of deliverance. The psalmist often depicts the time of distress as physical or spiritual dismay, most often the danger of death.

The cords of death encompassed me, And the torrents of ungodliness terrified me. The cords of Sheol surrounded me; The snares of death confronted me (Psalm 18:4,5, NASB)

In the minds of the psalmists, the power of death forcefully invaded life and pulled a person from the realm of the living to that of the dead—to Sheol. They personify Sheol as an aggressive force, binding people with cords (i.e. sickness or affliction), and pulling them into the bottomless pit.

On other occasions, the distress comes directly from God as punishment for sin.

Now as for me, I said in my prosperity, "I will never be moved." O LORD, by Your favor You have made my mountain to stand strong; You hid Your face, I was dismayed (Psalm 30:6,7, NASB).

When I kept silent about my sin, my body wasted away Through my groaning all day long. For day and night Your hand was heavy upon me; My vitality was drained away as with the fever heat of summer (Psalm 32:3,4, NASB).

The psalmist recognized that God punished sin, even among His own chosen people. Therefore, when calamity came, the psalmists searched their own hearts to see if the source of affliction resided with them. If so, repentance followed.

The role of Satan was not understood by the people of Israel when the psalms were written so he is never blamed for the psalmists' troubles. Satan clearly worked against God's people from the early pages of the Bible, but only later did they understand his role in the world. The words Satan and devil do not occur in the book of Psalms at all. The psalmists attribute all troubles to God, Sheol, or their enemies.

One obvious truth emerges as you read the distressing accounts in the many thanksgiving psalms: The psalmists never describe the details of what actually happened to them. They write in such general terms that their words could fit many situations. Look again at the examples in Psalms 18, 30, and 32. The psalmists never emphasize the details of past calamities, instead focusing on the deliverance God had provided.

Often, a brief, sincere cry to God bridges the gap between calamity and deliverance.

Praise as Thanksgiving

In my distress I called upon the LORD, And cried to my God for help; He heard my voice out of His temple, And my cry for help before Him came into His ears (Psalm 18:6, NASB).

To You, O LORD, I called, And to the LORD I made supplication: "What profit is there in my blood, if I go down to the pit? Will the dust praise You? Will it declare Your faithfulness? Hear, O LORD, and be gracious to me; O LORD, be my helper" (Psalm 30:8-10, NASB).

God controls every affair in your life and mine. When calamity comes—and it comes to everyone, sooner or later—we must cry out to God for help. The psalmist assures us that "God is our refuge and strength, A very present help in trouble" (Psalm 46:1 NASB). Our hope lies in Him who loved us from the very foundations of the world and who gave His only begotten Son that we might have life in Him. The psalmists cried out to this same God for deliverance.

The report of deliverance—the actual account of what God has done—follows the cry for help. This report appears in both the simplest and the most complex thanksgiving psalms. It declares the praise of God and boasts about His gracious acts.

God comes to the rescue of His servants with might and power.

Then the earth shook and quaked; And the foundations of the mountains were trembling And were shaken, because He was angry. Smoke went up out of His nostrils, And fire from His mouth devoured; Coals were kindled by it. He bowed the heavens also, and came down With thick darkness under His feet. He rode upon a cherub and flew; And He sped upon the wings of the wind (Psalm 18:7-10, NASB).

Lesson Two

When He arrives, He brings deliverance.

He sent from on high, He took me; He drew me out of many waters. He delivered me from my strong enemy, And from those who hated me, for they were too mighty for me (Psalm 18:16,17, NASB).

I sought the LORD, and He answered me, And delivered me from all my fears (Psalm 34:4, NASB

On the day I called You answered me; You made me bold with strength in my soul (Psalm 138:3, 6 NASB).

If sin caused the grief, God forgives it.

I acknowledged my sin to You, And my iniquity I did not hide; I said, "I will confess my transgressions to the LORD;" And You forgave the guilt of my sin (Psalm 32:5, NASB).

God can deliver from any sin or bondage. He deals with humankind graciously and powerfully. How can we do anything but praise His holy name?

BIBLE ASSIGNMENT

Read Psalm 116 and identify the report of deliverance and its specific elements.

_____
_____
_____
_____

Praise as Thanksgiving

_____
_____
_____
_____
_____

Your Exploration of the Text

Deliverance brings joy and joy leads to praise.

You have turned for me my mourning into dancing; You have loosed my sackcloth and girded me with gladness, That my soul may sing praise to You and not be silent. O LORD my God, I will give thanks to You forever (Psalm 30:11,12, NASB).

This psalm, like many of the thanksgiving psalms, concludes with a renewed vow to praise God.

The term *renewed* illustrates the relationship of the thanksgiving psalm to the psalm of lamentation. The lamentation psalm anticipates deliverance and the thanksgiving psalm celebrates it, fulfilling the original vow of praise from the lamentation psalm. These two types of psalms complement one another.

Why must the thanksgiving psalm renew the vow of praise? Here we see the inadequacy of the English word *thank* to depict the Hebrew idea of praise. Rather than praising God once for His gracious deeds, praise was ongoing; celebrated during annual celebrations such as the Feasts of Passover, Pentecost, and Tabernacles. Individuals certainly celebrated their own experiences of God's grace as well.

Many thanksgiving psalms conclude on a note of general praise of God. It appears more often in hymns rather than thanksgiving psalms, but occasionally concludes some thanksgiving psalms as if to fulfill the renewed vow of praise.

In summary, we find two things in the conclusion of the thanksgiving psalm: a renewed vow of praise and, sometimes, praise itself. We realize the continuous nature of praise in ancient Israel and the joy with which praise was expressed.

BIBLE ASSIGNMENT

Read Psalm 116:12-19 and note the renewed vow of praise found in its conclusion.

PRAISE AS THANKSGIVING

SELF-CHECK TEST

Choose the word from the list below which best completes each following statement.

deliverance	confessional	renewed
cry for help	descriptive	declarative
intention	distress	continuous

1. Common thanksgiving psalms begin with a statement of the psalmist's _____ to praise God.

2. The true nature of the thanksgiving psalm is _____, testifying to God's goodness before others.

3. Looking back at the time of _____ is usually the first part of the report of deliverance in a thanksgiving psalm.

4. The report of _____ appears in both the simplest and the most complex thanksgiving psalm.

5. The vow of praise at the end of a thanksgiving psalm is called the _____ vow of praise.

6. The conclusion of the thanksgiving psalm makes us realize the _____ nature of praise in ancient Israel.to change you in any way He desires and to direct you in how you might apply His Word to your life.

Lesson Three

Thanksgiving

A Path to Praise

Praise is the Rightful Response to God's Help (Psalm 30)

LESSON THREE

PSALM 30:1-12

PRAISE IS THE RIGHTFUL RESPONSE TO GOD'S HELP

Key Verse

You have turned for me my mourning into dancing; You have loosed my sackcloth and girded me with gladness (Psalm 30:11, NASB).

Introduction

You are about to begin a marvelous journey—that is, discovering God's Word through the inductive study method. As you **DISCOVER** (observe), **DISCERN** (interpret), and **DEVOTE** (apply) yourself to His Word, you will experience growth as a **DISCIPLE** of Christ (through commitment and obedience) and the Holy Spirit will guide, encourage, and teach you.

Lesson Three begins our study of specific thanksgiving psalms. The inductive Bible study process follows a well-defined pattern. If you have completed previous studies in the Enliven series, you will notice a great deal of continuity with your earlier studies. If this is your first time attempting inductive Bible study, you will be enriched by your discoveries. Lessons Three through Twelve will focus on specific psalms, all of which will lead you on a Path to Praise. Are you ready for the journey of a lifetime? Then let's get started!

Pause for Prayer

Begin each study with prayer and continue to pause for prayer as you diligently work through the lesson.

Blessed are those who keep His testimonies, who seek Him with the whole heart! (Psalm 119:2)

Start your journey at the throne of grace and give your heavenly Father praise for the gift of His holy Scriptures. Ask Him to teach you the truth through the power of the Holy Spirit as you study Psalm 30. Talk to Him in your own words about your desire to seek Him with your whole heart. Embrace the promise of His blessing as a result of your commitment to know His Word and keep it. As we write this study, we are lifting you up before the Father, recognizing that knowing God's word is the key to victorious living.

Psalm 30—Praise is the Rightful Response to God's Help

THE TEXT

Psalm 30:1-12

A Psalm. A Song at the dedication of the house of David.

¹I will extol You, O LORD, for You have lifted me up, And have not let my foes rejoice over me. ² O LORD my God, I cried out to You, And You healed me. ³ O LORD, You brought my soul up from the grave; You have kept me alive, that I should not go down to the pit. ⁴ Sing praise to the LORD, you saints of His, And give thanks at the remembrance of His holy name. ⁵ For His anger is but for a moment, His favor is for life; Weeping may endure for a night, But joy comes in the morning. ⁶ Now in my prosperity I said, "I shall never be moved." ⁷ LORD, by Your favor You have made my mountain stand strong; You hid Your face, and I was troubled. ⁸ I cried out to You, O LORD; And to

the LORD I made supplication: ⁹ "What profit is there in my blood, When I go down to the pit? Will the dust praise You? Will it declare Your truth? ¹⁰ Hear, O LORD, and have mercy on me; LORD, be my helper!" ¹¹ You have turned for me my mourning into dancing; You have put off my sackcloth and clothed me with gladness, ¹² To the end that my glory may sing praise to You and not be silent.

O LORD my God, I will give thanks to You forever.

DISCOVER

The best way to discover God's Word simply is to read, read, read! Begin by reading through our first thanksgiving psalm, Psalm 30, and meditating on it verse-by-verse. Notice the title given to this psalm as you begin reading. This will reinforce the authorship and the purpose of the psalm.

Read the psalm again and continue the observation process by asking the five W's and one H questions (Who? What? Why? When? Where? How?). You may not find answers for all the questions, but asking them helps lay the foundation for discovery. Don't write anything down yet. Just observe.

Psalm 30—Praise is the Rightful Response to God's Help

Finally, read the psalm a third time, keeping the five W's and one H questions in mind. This time, read the psalm aloud so that you will not only *see* it, but also hear it. Don't spend time analyzing the text, but you may want to make brief notes below with thoughts and questions that come to mind.

My Helping Questions and Answers

Lesson Three

Now that you have observed the text, briefly summarize what you have discovered. Just note the obvious. Discerning will come in the next section.

My Findings

_____
_____
_____
_____
_____
_____
_____
_____
_____

DISCERN

Every Text Has a Context

Now that you have an overview of the text, it is time to start looking at it more intentionally. It is important to keep in mind Lessons One and Two as you begin your study of the first of ten thanksgiving psalms.

Psalm 30—Praise is the Rightful Response to God's Help

1. In Lesson One, you learned that 116 of the 150 psalms have titles attached to them, which appear in the Hebrew text. What is the title assigned to Psalm 30?

2. You also learned that 101 psalms have statements of authorship. Who is the author of Psalm 30?

LESSON THREE

3. Who penned the words to this psalm? To whom is the psalm directed? Does it include a reference to any other person(s)? Identify the characters in this chapter.

___

4. To correctly interpret a scripture's meaning, you must know its context. From the information you have gleaned so far, can you determine the context, or environment, that surrounds Psalm 30? What occasion led to the singing of this psalm, according to its title? Who would be hearing it and singing it?

___

Psalm 30—Praise is the Rightful Response to God's Help

As you continue to study the text, you will discover answers to some of the other questions you have been asking. Why did David write this psalm? What is its purpose? Where was it sung? When was it sung? Considering the occasion and the probable number of people in attendance, how was the singing most likely orchestrated and presented? These questions may have come to your mind as you read and reread the text. Some answers are obvious and some will require further research at another time, but this is just the beginning.

_____
_____
_____
_____
_____
_____
_____
_____

Let's move to the next step in discerning this beautiful and historically important song of thanksgiving.

Marking the Text

To help you discern the meaning, go through the passage again applying Helping Tools: underlining, highlighting, or marking with symbols—key words, ideas, phrases, concepts, or anything that jumps out at you.

LESSON THREE

Keys Words Open the Door to Understanding

Key words are repeated terms or phrases that provide essential information needed to interpret a scripture text. Key words unlock the door of discernment and, because they are usually easy to recognize, identifying them happens early in the observation process.

For this exercise, you will need a set of erasable colored pencils for marking key words on the Scripture text at the beginning of this lesson. When you assign a shape (circle, square, rectangle, triangle, etc.) or icon (star, cross, crown, etc.) and a color to a key word, record it on a separate sheet of paper or an index card for easy reference throughout this study.

The Scripture text is double spaced to allow room for you to mark the text and make notations that are pertinent to the study. We suggest that you make notes in pencil so that any changes can be easily made.

1. Did you notice that LORD and God are repeated many times? These are key words, so you will want to pinpoint them and their pronouns by marking them with specific shapes or icons. For example, you could mark LORD and God with a red triangle.

    - How many times is LORD mentioned in Psalm 30, including pronouns (He, Him, etc.)?
    _____
    _____
    _____
    _____
    _____

Psalm 30—Praise is the Rightful Response to God's Help

- How many times is God mentioned?

_____
_____
_____
_____
_____

Although God is mentioned only twice, note that the psalmist refers to Him both times as "LORD my God," making His name very personal to David. Any time God's name is mentioned in the Bible, it is important. You should mark His name the same way throughout all your studies, creating a thread. Be sure to add these words to your list of key words.

2. Read the text again, looking for more key words. You may notice that the psalm is sung in the first person (I, me, my, etc.). Since these pronouns are used multiple times, mark them. You could use a blue rectangle to mark these words. When you count the number of times these pronouns are used, you will grasp their importance.

_____
_____
_____
_____
_____

LESSON THREE

3. You discovered from the title that the people who would be singing this psalm are the people of Israel attending the dedication of the Temple. Based on this observation, do these first-person pronouns refer to the psalmist or the people of Israel?

___

4. Verse 4 is addressed to "you saints of His." Reflect on this. Who are His saints in this song? Mark this pronoun in the Scripture text in the same way you marked the first-person pronouns.

___

5. While *praise* and its synonyms appear only a few times in the text, they are important words. The theme of the psalm centers around praise and thanksgiving. Therefore, mark praise(s) and thank(s). Also, mark extol in verse 1 because it is a synonym of praise. You could draw a green megaphone to mark these words.

Psalm 30—Praise is the Rightful Response to God's Help

6. Expressions of time usually explain when an event occurred. In Psalm 30, however, expressions of time are poetic in nature. Look for time references as you read the text again and mark those with a symbol, such as a brown circle, or highlight them with a certain color.

7. Read the psalm verse by verse, and look for contrasting, or opposite, words or phrases. When you discover them, put a bracket to the left of the verse(s) on your scripture worksheet and write "contrast."

Compile Lists

Lists make details come to life! The psalmist includes many details in his praise, as well as details about deeds of the LORD God. Using the chart below, write down each expression of the psalmist in the left column and every deed of the LORD in the right column. Put the verse number to the left of each entry for easy reference. We have included an example to get you started.

	The Psalmist's Expressions		**The LORD God's Deeds**
v.1	I will extol you	v.1	You have lifted me up You have not let my foes rejoice over me
v.2	I cried out to you	v.2	You healed me
		v.3	You brought my soul up from the grave
		v.3	You have kept me alive

The title tells us that David authored Psalm 30, and it was sung at the dedication of the temple. In question three, did you conclude that the personal pronouns (I, me, my) were referring to the people of Israel? Just imagine the people of Israel making the words of this song their own as they sang to the LORD their God!

Pause for Prayer

You have commanded us To keep Your precepts diligently (Psalm 119:4).

To keep God's precepts, we first must know them. Through the exercises in this lesson, you have begun to discern, or interpret, Psalm 30. You have learned its authorship and purpose. Perhaps you were able to envision the multitude of Israel's worshippers blending their voices together in song as an offering of praise to the LORD their God. As you begin "pulling it all together," ask God to open

Psalm 30—Praise is the Rightful Response to God's Help

your heart and your mind to see the big picture. Seek the guidance of the Holy Spirit. Welcome Him as He comes alongside you, and allow Him to teach you His character.

Pulling It All Together

1. You have invested time in observing this psalm and now it's time to put into practice what you learned in Lesson Two. Read the psalm paragraph by paragraph, looking for the various elements of a thanksgiving psalm. Label each element in the text. In the chart below, write the verse(s) where each element is found.

Element	Verse
The Title	
Intent to Praise	
Introductory Summary This follows the intent to praise and includes a summary of why God is being praised.	

Element	Verse	
Report of Deliverance This is the main body of the thanksgiving psalm. The psalmist looks back on his time of distress, remembers his cry to God for help, and reports God's gracious deliverance. First, designate the verses included in the overall report of deliverance. Then, designate the verses for each of the categories: distress, cry for help, and deliverance.	Overall Report of Deliverance	
	Distress	
	Cry for Help	
	Deliverance	
Renewed Vow of Praise The final element of the thanksgiving psalm expresses a promise of continued praise for God's gracious acts.		

2. Review the heading and key verse at the beginning of this lesson. The heading reflects the main focus of the chapter, and the key verse is the portion of the Scriptural text that best articulates that focus. In your printed text of Psalm 30, in a color of your choice, draw a box around the key verse. Review the text and think about why this heading and this verse were chosen to sum up the essence of this chapter. You may want to come up with your own secondary heading. If so, write it below.

_____

_____

_____

Psalm 30—Praise is the Rightful Response to God's Help

_____
_____
_____
_____
_____

3. Prayerfully read Psalm 30 again and, as you do, write aspects of God's character in the margin alongside the applicable verses. Later, you can transfer them to the margin of your Bible. As you read Psalm 30 in the future, these descriptive words about your God will help you recall all you learned in this study.

Open Your Tool Box

Up to this point, you have internalized Psalm 30 by reading the text several times, discovering truths from your own observations apart from outside sources. There lies the beauty of the inductive study method. You consulted no outside sources until now, but here at the end of your study, you have the freedom to explore commentaries, concordances, and other resources. Dig deeper and compare what you have learned with what Bible scholars have to say. You can fill your tool box at the library, on the internet, or perhaps from your own collection of publications.

Did you notice that LORD in this text is in all upper-case letters? A word study of LORD will give insight as to why. An exhaustive concordance serves as a helpful tool when doing a word study. Let's take a look at how it works.

Lesson Three

Scripture refers to God by many different names. By studying the meaning of those names, you will gain a clearer view of how David and the Israelites understood His character.

Let us go to the Hebrew section of The New Strong's Exhaustive Concordance of the Bible, one of many exhaustive concordances. The following definitions have been excerpted from Strong's, and the reference number from the Hebrew dictionary in that concordance is identified. Note that the first words for God and LORD are in Hebrew and the phonetic pronunciations follow.

- *God*: Yehôvâh, *yeh-ho-vaw'*; (the) self-Existent or Eternal; Jehovah, Jewish national name of God:—Jehovah, the Lord. (*Strong's* 3068, compare to 3050)

- *LORD*: Yâhh, *yaw...Jah*, the sacred name:—the Lord, most vehement. (*Strong's* 3050, contraction from 3068)

It is noted that *LORD* (*Yâhh*) is a shortened form of *Y^ehôvâh*, meaning the same.

When David calls out to the LORD, he is calling out to God (Jehovah). Whenever you see LORD in scripture, you know that it means Jehovah.

What significance could this double expression of God's name have on interpreting the text?

_____

_____

_____

Psalm 30—Praise is the Rightful Response to God's Help

_____
_____
_____
_____

My Interpretation

You now have an idea of Psalm 30's historical purpose. It's time to prayerfully consider what this thanksgiving psalm meant to David and the people of Israel. Review the text again and briefly summarize it as if you were explaining it to another person. Putting your interpretation on paper will reinforce what you have learned and organize it in your mind. Remember to keep your explanation within context, that is, the environment in which this beautiful psalm was sung. Record your summary below.

_____
_____
_____
_____
_____
_____
_____
_____
_____

LESSON THREE

DEVOTE

Through this study, you have made an investment in your walk with the Lord. As you encounter Psalm 30 in the future, you may glean new insight. But for now, take a few moments reflect on how this passage of scripture speaks to you personally. Write down your thoughts, perhaps as a prayer. Listen to the voice of the Spirit. God will speak to you as you engage with His Word. You may want to begin a journal of thanksgiving on the lines below. This is where you take ownership of the text—consider it as God's gift to you.

Psalm 30—Praise is the Rightful Response to God's Help

Pause for Prayer

You have dealt well with Your servant, O LORD, according to Your word. Teach me good judgment and knowledge, For I believe Your commandments (Psalm 119:65, 66, NKJV).

Through prayer, we engage with the Spirit of God. We talk to God, but we also listen to the voice of the Spirit. Allow the Spirit to give you additional insights about Psalm 30. Is God speaking to you personally through this psalm? If so, write about it in the space below.

_____
_____
_____
_____
_____
_____

You have studied Psalm 30 deliberately, carefully trusting God for discernment all along the way. As you complete the final, personal component of this lesson, do so with a heart of thanksgiving.

DISCIPLE

Discipleship closely follows devotion. You interpreted this scripture, applied its lessons to your heart, and allowed the Holy Spirit to speak personally to you. Out of that prayerful reflection must come a response. What will I do with all I have learned?

LESSON THREE

Psalm 30:5 reveals that God's "favor is for life." Read the hymn recorded in Psalm 103:1-5 and reflect on God's blessing in your lifetime.

Has He forgiven your iniquities? Extol Him for His grace and mercy and commit to mirror that grace and mercy in your life to draw others to Him.

Has He healed your diseases and redeemed your life from destruction? Praise Him and respond by sharing your testimony to encourage others.

Has He crowned you with lovingkindness and tender mercies and satisfied your mouth with good things? Count your blessings daily and accept them with joy and gratitude.

When you overcome negative thoughts by meditating on His goodness, may you find that your youth is renewed like the eagle's.

Return to Psalm 30 and peruse it stanza by stanza. Perhaps you would like to sing the lyrics to your own tune. Dwell on who God is—His character—and prayerfully decide how you will respond to your LORD God, the eternal one. Now write your commitment below.

_____
_____
_____
_____
_____

Psalm 30—Praise is the Rightful Response to God's Help

_____
_____
_____
_____

Congratulations! You just finished your first inductive study of a thanksgiving psalm. Remember that God's Word is unfathomable. That's why we keep studying it "precept upon precept… line upon line, Here a little, there a little" (Isaiah 28:13). Are you excited about moving on to your study of Psalm 21?

Enliven Encountering God through His Word

Lesson Four

Thanksgiving

A Path to Praise

God's Strength Brings Joy and Praise (Psalm 21)

LESSON FOUR

PSALM 21

GOD'S STRENGTH BRINGS JOY AND PRAISE

Key Verse

Be exalted, O LORD, in Your own strength! We will sing and praise Your power (Psalm 21:13).

Introduction

Through discipline and perseverance, with the direction of the Holy Spirit, you engaged in a detailed study of Psalm 30. What a comfort to know that God turns your mourning into dancing and clothes you with gladness! In this lesson, you will practice your inductive study skills and build upon what you have learned as you dive into Psalm 21. You will renew your mind as God's character comes to the forefront of this beautifully written psalm filled with thanksgiving from a different perspective than that of Psalm 30.

Remember that you are learning "precept upon precept… line upon line, Here a little, there a little" (Isaiah 28:13). Try to spend some time each day studying your lesson—say, no more than an hour—rather than trying to get as much done as you can in one sitting. Also, keep in mind that this is just the beginning. The Holy Spirit is laying a foundation for further insights into Psalm 21 in the future.

Your Exploration of the Text

Pause for Prayer

Your testimonies I have taken as a heritage forever, For they are the rejoicing of my heart (Psalm 119:111).

Before you delve into Scripture, bow before its author. Enter His gates with thanksgiving by praying Psalm 100. Make it more personal by inserting first-person pronouns into the text (I will, I know, etc.).

Express your desire to truly know Him through His word. Ask Him to enlighten your darkness through His proven word (Psalm 18:28, 30) Express what you hope to gain through spending time in Psalm 21. Then continue on your journey of discovery. Remember that you have been covered in prayer for every step of your journey.

PSALM 21—GOD'S STRENGTH BRINGS JOY AND PRAISE

THE TEXT

Psalm 21:1-13 (NKJV)

To the Chief Musician. A Psalm of David.

¹The king shall have joy in Your strength, O LORD; And in Your salvation how greatly shall he rejoice! ² You have given him his heart's desire, And have not withheld the request of his lips. Selah

³ For You meet him with the blessings of goodness; You set a crown of pure gold upon his head. ⁴ He asked life from You, and You gave it to him—Length of days forever and ever. ⁵ His glory is great in Your salvation; Honor and majesty You have placed upon him. ⁶ For You have made him most blessed forever; You have made him exceedingly glad with Your presence. ⁷ For the king trusts in the LORD, And through the mercy of the Most High he shall not be moved. ⁸ Your hand will find all

Your enemies; Your right hand will find those who hate You. ⁹ You shall make them as a fiery oven in the time of Your anger; The LORD shall swallow them up in His wrath, And the fire shall devour them. ¹⁰ Their offspring You shall destroy from the earth, And their descendants from among the sons of men. ¹¹ For they intended evil against You; They devised a plot which they are not able to perform.

¹² Therefore You will make them turn their back; You will make ready Your arrows on Your string toward their faces. ¹³ Be exalted, O LORD, in Your own strength! We will sing and praise Your power.

DISCOVER

As you learned last time, studying God's word inductively means observing the Scripture text for yourself. Inductive means "drawn into" or "to be led into." **Discovery** draws you into the word by the power of the Holy Spirit, leading you into truth. Begin by prayerfully reading Psalm 21. Be sure to notice the title when you begin reading. Read thoughtfully, asking "What does the psalm say?" You will ask "What does the psalm mean?" in the **Discern** section.

Psalm 21—God's Strength Brings Joy and Praise

Next, read the psalm again, asking the helping questions (Who? What? Why? When? Where? How?). Do not write anything down just yet. Just observe, observe, observe.

Read the text a third time, keeping the helping questions in mind. Do not get bogged down if you cannot find all the answers. Each question may not be relevant to this passage. This time, read the text aloud so that you do not only see it, but you hear it. Do not start analyzing, but write down any obvious observations that come to mind as you read, along with your helping questions and answers

My Helping Questions and Answers

_____
_____
_____
_____
_____
_____
_____
_____
_____
_____
_____
_____

Lesson Four

Summary. Now that you have observed the text, briefly summarize your discoveries. Just note the obvious. Discerning will come in the next section.

My Findings

Every Text Has a Context

Now that you have read and re-read Psalm 21, questions undoubtedly have come to your mind. Start filling in the blanks by referring back to Lessons One and Two.

Psalm 21—God's Strength Brings Joy and Praise

1. Identify the author of Psalm 21.

2. The title reveals that David addressed this psalm to a specific person. Who is that person?

3. Who are the lead characters? Who are the supporting characters?

4. What title would the Chief Musician probably hold today?

Lesson Four

In the **DISCERN** section, we will take a closer look at some details about the music ministry in Israel's worship.

After prayerfully reading and re-reading Psalm 21, carefully observing, and asking questions, you could stop right here and be blessed. But in these 13 verses, a treasure trove waits to be uncovered! Digging deeper will provide an invaluable reward in your walk with the Lord. So roll up your sleeves and begin to mine the treasures that are waiting for you. As you do your part, allow the Holy Spirit to do His.

DISCERN

Key Words Open the Door to Understanding

Now it's time to get out your colored pencils and identify the passage's key words. Let this be a creative exercise. Do you have the list of key words that notes the way you chose to mark them in Lesson Three? Some of the same words will appear in this lesson. For easy reference, label your first set of key words "Psalm 30" and begin a new list for Psalm 21, transferring words that are repeated, along with the colors, shapes, or icons you used. This allows for consistency throughout your study of the thanksgiving psalms, as well as future studies.

Psalm 21—God's Strength Brings Joy and Praise

1. You probably identified LORD as a leading character in Psalm 21. So mark the word LORD, along with its pronouns (You, Your, etc.) on your Scripture text as you did in Lesson Three.

   To emphasize just how important the LORD is in these 13 verses, record how many times He is mentioned in the passage.

   _____
   _____
   _____
   _____

2. Re-read the text, looking for more key words. You most likely observed that the king is another lead character. Of course, a king must have a kingdom. What nation would this king rule over?

   _____
   _____
   _____
   _____

3. Although the nation of Israel is not named in this text, we know this king rules over that nation. Choose a color to identify Israel and its synonyms throughout the Bible. You could choose to mark it with a royal blue star. Save that thought for future studies. Since the king in this psalm is the king of Israel, you could mark all references to him with a royal blue crown. Once you have finished marking your text, count how many times the king and his synonyms are found.

LESSON FOUR

4. In verse 8, another group of people is introduced. Mark that as a key word, along with its pronouns in the verses that follow, perhaps with a brown rectangle. Record how many times that word is used.

- Identifying characters helps you discern the author's message. You are well on your way to a deeper understanding of Psalm 21.

5. Verses 8-12 declare what God will do to His enemies. Five different words describe His actions. Mark them all the same way, such as with red flames.

Psalm 21—God's Strength Brings Joy and Praise

6. Reading the text again, you will find three references to time. Mark those as you did in Lesson Three.

7. Read Psalm 21 again and look for contrasting (opposite) words or phrases. When you discover them, put a bracket to the left of the verse(s) and write "contrast." You might discover that entire passages contrast with one another. Record below any contrasts you find. Be sure to indicate the reference for each contrast. If you find contrasting passages, simply summarize them rather than writing out multiple verses.

Lesson Four

Compile Lists

Compiling a list about a given subject helps organize details about it. Do you see information about the king and the LORD in this psalm that you can organize into lists? Record what you discover about each of them on the chart below. Put the verse number to the left of each entry for easy reference. We have included an example to get you started.

	The King		The LORD
v.1	Shall have joy	v.1	In the LORD's strength
v.1	Shall rejoice	v.1	In the LORD's salvation
		v.2	Has given the king his heart's desire
		v.2	Has not withheld the request of the king's lips

Psalm 21—God's Strength Brings Joy and Praise

1. Who is the recipient of blessings in each of these verses?

   _____

   _____

   _____

   _____

- Record below what you observe about God and His enemies.

	The LORDs Enemies		The LORD
		v.8	His hand will find all His enemies
		v.8	His right hand will find those who hate Him
v.9	Will become as a fiery oven in the time of the LORD's anger	v.9	Will make His enemies as a fiery oven in the time of His anger
		v.2	

Notice that God's enemies were, indeed, the king's enemies. They devised plots against the king, and, therefore, against God. While ultimate glory for defeating the enemies went to the LORD, He used the king as His divine agent to accomplish His will. Some versions of the Bible, such as the New King James Version, attribute certain pronouns to God by capitalizing them, while other versions attribute them to the king by using lower case. The original Hebrew text did not utilize capitalization. Therefore, in situations involving God and His anointed king of Israel, there is a fine line in designating the pronouns precisely and attributing behaviors and traits to God or the king. This will be addressed further in the "Pulling It All Together" section.

Terms of Cause and Effect

Terms like "for," "therefore," "this reason," and "so that" are called terms of cause and effect. They indicate that there is a relationship between two passages of Scripture. When you see these terms, go back to the preceding verse(s) to establish the relationship between the verses. Look for terms of cause and effect in verses 1-7, and underline or circle them in the text. On the chart below, record each cause in the left column and each effect in the right column, underlining the term of cause and effect. Be sure to include the verse reference.

Cause	Effect

Psalm 21—God's Strength Brings Joy and Praise

Has this exercise given you insight into reasons for the king's gratitude toward the LORD? How has God given the king his heart's desire? What did God give him when he asked for life? Notice that verses 1-6 culminate in verse 7. As a result of the LORD's provisions, anointing, and promises, what does the king declare?

_____
_____
_____
_____
_____
_____

Now outline the terms of cause and effect in verses 8-12.

Cause	Effect

Your chart reveals the attitude of God's (and the king's) enemies toward Him and the resulting consequences. Given their behavior and results, would you want to pattern your attitude after that of the king or God's enemies?

Pause for Prayer

Forever, O LORD, Your word is settled in heaven. Your faithfulness endures to all generations; You established the earth, and it abides (Psalm 119:89, 90).

Through prayer and commitment, you have affirmed that the desire of your heart is to know God through His Word and His presence. No matter what your circumstances, the changes for better or worse in your life, in good times and in bad times, you can be certain that God's Word never changes and He is faithful. You can proactively commit to trust in the Lord and not be moved. If you are a believer in Jesus Christ, you have the Holy Spirit within you to teach you and guide you into all truth. As John 14:26 proclaims, the Holy Spirit is your Helper who "will teach you all things." As you come

Psalm 21—God's Strength Brings Joy and Praise

before your heavenly Father now, express in your own words the essence of what He has taught you in this lesson so far. Ask Him for help and guidance to "pull it all together" through the power of the Holy Spirit.

Pulling It All Together

1. You will recall from Lesson Two that the three components for a thanksgiving psalm are the intent to praise God, the report of deliverance, and the renewed vow of praise. As you review the text, identify these three elements in Psalm 21, including the location of the verses that relate to each element.

Element	Verse Locations
Intent to Praise God	
Report of Deliverance	
Renewed Vow of Praise	

These elements are not as detailed in Psalm 21 as they were in Psalm 30. However, they qualify to categorize Psalm 21 as a thanksgiving psalm. This is one of eleven psalms that have been designated as Royal Psalms by Bible scholars. The king ruled over the nation of Israel, God's chosen people, and the king was chosen and anointed by God. Therefore, it is not surprising that certain Royal Psalms were written specifically for special occasions in the king's life, such as the king's coronation, his marriage, and his engagement in battle.

The king in ancient Israel was understood to be God's human agent to lead His people. God ruled as the ultimate King of Israel, but His rule was carried out by an Israelite king. The Davidic Covenant (2 Samuel 7) sealed kingship in Israel. As God's anointed leader, the king was to be righteous, gracious, and just in all his decisions and actions. As God's agent, he would be victorious in battle against God's enemies. Psalm 21 reveals the close relationship between the God and the king in Israel. Other Royal Psalms focus on the importance of Israel's king. Psalm 2 describes a king who is totally submitted to God. Psalm 72 emphasizes the righteous rule of a godly king.

2. Review the heading and key verse at the beginning of this lesson. Reflect on them as you carefully read the chapter again. Identify the key verse on the Scripture text by drawing a box around it, using the same color that you used in Lesson Three to pinpoint the key verse. This will give you continuity throughout your study so that you can quickly find each key verse.

Write God's attributes alongside each verse in the margin of your text, just as you did in Lesson Three. Later, transfer those to the margin of your Bible.

Open Your Tool Box

Let us dig deeper to discover more about this psalm. Now that you have started discerning (or interpreting) the text on your own, it's time to look to outside sources for additional understanding. First, we will return to *The New Strong's Exhaustive Concordance of the Bible.*

Psalm 21—God's Strength Brings Joy and Praise 105

1. Verse 2 ends with a word that is strange to our vocabulary, *Selah*. *Strong's* sheds some light on this word.

   - *Selah*: celâh, *seh-law*; suspension (of music), i.e. pause. (*Strong's* 5542)

   Will this change the way you transition from verse 2 to verse 3?

2. Notice how David begins and ends the psalm. What word does he use in the first and last verses that gives us insight into God's character? What is his final praise to the LORD?

   _____

   _____

   _____

   _____

   _____

Let us explore the meaning of strength and power in *Strong's*. The following definitions and phonetic pronunciations have been excerpted from Strong's and the reference number from the Hebrew dictionary in that concordance is identified.

- *strength*: 'ôz, *oze*; or (fully) owz, *oze*; ... strength in various applications (force, security, majesty, praise):—boldness, loud, might, power, strength, strong. (*Strong's* 5797)

- *power*: gebûwrâh, *gheb-oo-raw'*; force (literal or figurative); by implication valor, victory:—force, mastery, might, mighty, (tact, power), power, strength. (*Strong's* 1369)

Lesson Four

Notice that *strength* and *power* are very similar in meaning. Add them to your key word list and mark both words in the same way, such as with a red, jagged streak of lightning.

Why would God's strength and power be important enough to the king that the psalmist would begin and conclude his psalm by praising God for them?

_____
_____
_____
_____
_____

Cross-Referencing

Cross-referencing illuminates one Scripture through studying another Scripture. Since this psalm is directed to the Chief Musician, we can use cross-referencing to learn more about other musicians and musical leaders. In Lesson One, you learned about David's establishment of the temple singers in 1 Chronicles 15:16. Read 1 Chronicles 15:16-24; 25:1-7. Record your observations in the space below.

_____
_____
_____
_____

Psalm 21—God's Strength Brings Joy and Praise

_____
_____
_____
_____
_____
_____
_____
_____
_____
_____

A reputable Bible dictionary is another good resource for shedding light on various biblical topics in a concise, easy-to-understand way. A good choice would be *The Zondervan Pictorial Bible Dictionary* or *The Westminster Dictionary of the Bible*. If you do not own a Bible dictionary, you could borrow one from a local church library or the public library.

My Interpretation

In a court of law, a judge comes to a conclusion about resolving a case in many different ways. One of the most important means is through discovery. He or she learns a great deal through this procedure that can take months, or even years. After praying, the first thing you did was make observations about Psalm 21 by asking helping questions and establishing context. You used a variety of tools and study techniques to gain understanding of what the psalm means. Most importantly, you sought the guidance of the Holy Spirit. You are ready now to make your own judgment of the psalmist's intended meaning. Review your research of Psalm 21 and succinctly record your findings below.

_____
_____
_____
_____
_____
_____
_____
_____
_____
_____

DEVOTE

One of the most rewarding benefits of inductive Bible study is internalizing Scripture for your own spiritual growth. God's Word speaks.

Quieten your heart and let God's Word speak to you. Take your pen and record how God speaks to you through the king's testimony of God's character and victory over their enemies. "Be still, and

Psalm 21—God's Strength Brings Joy and Praise

know that I am God; I will be exalted among the nations, I will be exalted in the earth!" (Psalm 46:10, NIV).

Pause for Prayer

My soul melts from heaviness; Strengthen me according to Your word. I have chosen the way of truth; Your judgments I have laid before me (Psalm 119:28, 30).

You most likely observed from your study that the king exalted God for His strength and sang praises of His power. The king saw God's strength demonstrated through benefits toward him and vengeance toward His enemies. Take time to praise God, as the psalmist did, for His honor, goodness, and strength, even in your weakness. Thank Him for His judgments that are founded in truth. Laud Him as the mighty

Warrior who comes against the enemy of your soul and lift Him up as the Lord of your life who heaps blessings—tangible and intangible—upon you. Wait upon the Holy Spirit and let the Word speak.

What is God saying to you through His Word?

_____
_____
_____
_____
_____
_____
_____
_____
_____

DISCIPLE

Commitment. It takes time and energy. It requires devotion and dedication. "Commit your works to the Lord, And your thoughts will be established" (Proverbs 16:3). By engaging in this inductive study, you have committed time and energy to a worthwhile endeavor that will establish you in God's Word. Your commitment does not stop here. Will you apply all you've learned to make a difference in a broken world—a world whose leaders often do not acknowledge the sovereign ruler of the universe in their governments, laws, and decisions? How will you live in an when everyone seems to do what is "right in his own eyes" (Judges 17:6)?

In a quiet place, meditate on Psalm 21 verse by verse. Thoughtfully read it or sing it to your own tune as you complete this lesson. Compare your nation and its leaders to Israel and her king at the time this psalm was written. Do not forget to pause (*Selah*) at the end of verse 2. Prayerfully ask God what you can do to make a constructive difference for the glory of God in your sphere of influence—your family, friends, church, workplace, and community. Your scope may reach beyond the obvious. That is between you and God. The Greek word for *power* in the New Testament is *dunamis*. Part of the *Strong's* concordance definition is "can do." Dream big, and list the possibilities through the enabling power of the Holy Spirit. What can you do to make an impact in your corner of the world and beyond?

Reflect on our discussion in the Discern section about the anointed king as God's agent. What is your role as an agent of God in your culture?

_____

_____

_____

_____

_____

_____

_____

What a joy to have a royal thanksgiving psalm—a psalm written several thousand years ago for a king and, most likely, by a king—speak to you today! That is the power of God's Word. That is the power of the Holy Spirit: He preserved the truth of the Word so you can learn and grow from it today.

Are you ready to explore Psalm 32? It's an adventure you do not want to miss!

Lesson Five

Thanksgiving

A Path to Praise

God's Forgiveness is Joy Forevermore (Psalm 32)

LESSON FIVE

PSALM 32

GOD'S FORGIVENESS IS JOY FOREVERMORE

Key Verse

Be glad in the LORD and rejoice, you righteous; And shout for joy, all you upright in heart! (Psalm 32:11).

Introduction

Under the guidance of the Holy Spirit, you have dedicated yourself to a deep study of Psalms 30 and 21. You discovered that the first was a song at the dedication of the house of David—a rightful response of praise for God's help. The second was written by David and addressed to the Chief Musician to testify to the way God's strength brings joy and praise.

Now you will explore a different type of thanksgiving psalm. Like Psalm 21, Psalm 32 focuses on joy. David authored the psalm, labeled as "A Contemplation." Some translations of the Bible, label it a "Maskil." This word probably sounds familiar because it was defined in Lesson One of this study. We will look closer at the term when we open our tool box.

Your Exploration of the Text

Pause for Prayer

I will meditate on Your precepts, And contemplate Your ways. I will delight myself in Your statutes; I will not forget Your word (Psalm 119:15, 16).

Take time now to seek your heavenly Father's face. Praise Him for help in times of trouble and strength in your weakness. Ask Him to give you understanding as you draw near to Him through His holy Word.

Have you experienced times when you felt you had lost your joy? Do you have challenges competing with your thoughts today? Tell Him about it. Are you mentally or physically tired? Ask Him to renew your mind and body. Commit this time of study to Him for His glory. Then go to work! Do your part and the Holy Spirit will do His part.

PSALM 32—GOD'S FORGIVENESS IS JOY FOREVERMORE

THE TEXT

Psalm 32:1-11

A Psalm of David. A Contemplation.

¹ Blessed is he whose transgression is forgiven, Whose sin is covered. ² Blessed is the man to whom the LORD does not impute iniquity, And in whose spirit there is no deceit. ³ When I kept silent, my bones grew old Through my groaning all the day long. ⁴ For day and night Your hand was heavy upon me; My vitality was turned into the drought of summer. Selah ⁵ I acknowledged my sin to You, And my iniquity I have not hidden. I said, "I will confess my transgressions to the LORD," And You forgave the iniquity of my sin. Selah ⁶ For this cause everyone who is godly shall pray to You In a time when You may be found; Surely in a flood of great waters They shall not come near him.

7 You are my hiding place; You shall preserve me from trouble; You shall surround me with songs of deliverance. Selah [8] I will instruct you and teach you in the way you should go; I will guide you with My eye. [9] Do not be like the horse or like the mule, Which have no understanding, Which must be harnessed with bit and bridle, Else they will not come near you. [10] Many sorrows shall be to the wicked; But he who trusts in the LORD, mercy shall surround him. [11] Be glad in the LORD and rejoice, you righteous; And shout for joy, all you upright in heart!

DISCOVER

The title of Psalm 32 reveals its nature. It is contemplative. That word conveys quiet meditation, thoughtful observation or consideration, and reflection. So find yourself a quiet place. Perhaps you could sit outside as your senses come alive to the sound of birds singing, the sight of fluttering butterflies, and the touch of a gentle breeze. If it is too cold or humid outside, sit by a window and observe God's creation. Go to your own special place. Begin to contemplate the thoughtful words of

Psalm 32—God's Forgiveness is Joy Forevermore

David's psalm. It has been preserved through the ages for you.

Observing the Text

1. Read Psalm 32 with the purpose of discovering truth. You know what comes next. Who? What? Why? When? Where? How? Ask these helping questions as you read the text.

2. Carefully read the psalm a second time, continuing to saturate your mind with David's words. Note that several passages conclude with the word Selah. Pause and reflect on what you just read.

3. Read the psalm aloud now. What is the psalmist contemplating? Who are the main characters? How is he feeling? Why does he feel that way? As you read, record your observations by writing down your helping questions and answers.

My Helping Questions and Answers

_____
_____
_____
_____
_____
_____
_____

Summary. Briefly summarize your observations below.

My Findings

Psalm 32—God's Forgiveness is Joy Forevermore

_____
_____
_____

Every Text Has a Context

In this section, identify your observations to lay the foundation for discerning, or interpreting, Psalm 32. This is intentionally repetitive. You have probably experienced the feeling of seeing something new in God's Word – something you had never noticed before. That is one of the benefits of repetition, a feature of inductive study.

1. First, identify this psalm's author.
_____
_____
_____
_____

2. The title reveals that this psalm is a contemplation. Is David expressing his own thoughts or the thoughts of someone else? How do you know?
_____
_____
_____
_____

3. To whom is David directing his thoughts?

_____
_____
_____
_____

Are you ready to dig deeper? Let's move on to the Discern section. Remember, you are not alone. The Holy Spirit will bring the Scriptures alive as you pursue truth.

DISCERN

Key Words Open the Door to Understanding

The key words in Psalm 32 illustrate the depth of David's thoughts. Sharpen your colored pencils and begin your search. Look for words or phrases that the author uses repeatedly. Some are expressed in different forms but have the same meaning. This is a challenge that will make you think! You may mark these similar words with the same color and/or icon.

1. Walk through these verses several times, adding key words and phrases to your list of key words and marking them with the colors and/or icons of your choice. Remember to transfer similar words from your previous key word lists.

Psalm 32—God's Forgiveness is Joy Forevermore

_____
_____
_____
_____

2. As you know, any mention of God and His name is important. Marking those references will give you a thread to follow throughout Scripture. Record how many times God (including pronouns) is mentioned in these eleven verses. Are you amazed at the number of times David mentions Him in this short meditation?

_____
_____
_____
_____
_____
_____
_____

3. Mark any time references in the text. These provide a glimpse into the desperate nature of David's thoughts.

4. As you review the psalm verse by verse, search for words or phrases that are opposites. When you discover them, put a bracket to the left of the verse(s) in the text and write "contrast." Record those contrasts in the space below, along with the scripture reference. While "day and night" may

seem to be a contrast, that is not the case here. David is simply expressing that God's hand was heavy upon him both day and night.

The words "but," "however," and "nevertheless" offer clues that two different things are being compared. If you find such a word, underline it.

_____
_____
_____
_____
_____
_____
_____

Compile Lists

If you are a list maker, you probably find yourself mentally making lists as you read through a Scripture passage. Lists are a natural way to organize material so that it makes sense. Did you notice that David is contemplating two categories of people in this text? He includes himself in both groups. Categorize what you learn under the following headings. Be sure to include the verse reference to the left of your discovery. Verses 1 and 3 are examples of phrases that apply to the forgiven and the unforgiven.

Psalm 32—God's Forgiveness is Joy Forevermore

	The Forgiven		The Unforgiven
v.1	Blessed—transgression is forgiven	v.3	Kept silent
v.1	Sin is covered	v.3	Bones grew old

Do you see why David included himself in both groups? Write your conclusions below.

_____

_____

_____

_____

_____

LESSON FIVE

_____
_____
_____
_____
_____
_____

Did this exercise show you the progression of David's thoughts? Next to each verse reference below, write "happy" or "sad" (or draw an emotion face) to show your understanding of David's emotions as they evolved.

Verse	Emotion	Verse	Emotion
1		7	
2		8	
3		9	
4		10a	
5		10b	
6		11	

Can you identify with David's range of emotions? Have you ever experienced something similar in times of reflection?

Terms of Cause and Effect

Identify terms of cause and effect in the text. Examples include "for," "therefore," "for this reason," and "so that." When you see these terms, go back to the preceding verse(s) to find the cause-and-effect relationship. On the chart below, write the cause in the left column and the result in the right column, underlining the term of cause and effect. Be sure to include the verse for easy reference.

Cause	Effect

Pause for Prayer

Before I was afflicted I went astray, But now I keep Your word. You are good, and do good; Teach me Your statutes (Psalm 119:67, 68).

We all fail at times, resulting in a fractured relationship with God and disappointment with ourselves. At such times, our hearts may feel empty and depleted of joy. If we follow David's example and respond to the convicting power of the Holy Spirit, God forgives us and we can feel whole again. Perhaps you sense a need to do that right now before moving into the next segment of the lesson. Ask Him to replace that empty space with joy. Whether or not you feel the need to do this, you can rejoice in the knowledge that God is your hiding place and surrounds you with songs of deliverance. Express your gratitude to Him for instructing, teaching, and guiding you throughout this study so far. Tell Him that you trust Him to help you "pull it all together" in your pursuit of knowing Him.

Pulling It All Together

1. You are becoming familiar with the pattern of identifying the elements of a thanksgiving psalm. While the basic components are always present, each psalm varies in organization. Do not get bogged down in structure, but do your best as you look for the verse or verses that make up each element. You will notice that Psalm 32 does not include a renewed vow of praise, as such. Rather, David concludes with an exhortation.

Element	Verse Locations
Intent to Priase	
Distress	
Cry for Help	
Deliverance	
Exhortation (no vow)	

When you recognize these elements, you can see the progression of David's contemplation. Re-read the verses you listed above to appreciate how his words flow from one thought to the next.

2. If you have accepted Jesus as your Savior and asked His forgiveness from sin, you have been made righteous and upright in heart by His blood shed on the cross. You have every reason to rejoice and shout for joy! "Be glad in the LORD and rejoice, you righteous; And shout for joy, all you upright in heart!" (Psalm 32:11). Draw a box around that verse in the text.

3. As you discovered, this psalm includes many references to God. List His attributes alongside each verse in the margin of your text. If you take the time to transfer this information to the margin of your Bible for each of these psalms, you will be able to quickly spot God's attributes in your future Bible reading.

Open Your Tool Box

1. At the beginning of the Discern section, you were challenged to watch for words and phrases that appear in different forms but have the same meaning. Several words that fall in this category include b*lessed, songs, glad, rejoice,* and *joy. Blessed* is often understood as meaning "consecrated, sanctified, set apart." Let's seek a further understanding of what the word blessed means in Hebrew. Once again, we turn to *The New Strong's Exhaustive Concordance of the Bible*.

   - *Blessed*: ʼesher, *eh'-sher*; happiness; …how happy!—blessed, happy. (*Strong's* 835)

This provides great insight into David's description of how a person feels when transgressions are forgiven and sins are covered. Take a moment now to rejoice with your own song of deliverance because of your standing with God.

2. Another word usage that might bring a question to your mind is found in verse 2. "Blessed is the man to whom the LORD does not impute iniquity." You may wonder about the meaning of the uncommon word *impute*. The *Merriam-Webster Dictionary* defines the word as, "to lay responsibility or blame for." *Strong's* could offer additional clarity, as could a modern translation of paraphrase of the text.

When using inductive Bible study, it is advisable to use a version of the Bible that is a *translation* rather than a *paraphrase*. In a translation, a team of scholars puts the original Greek and Hebrew text into today's language to make it understandable. For example, 119 translators worked together on the *New King James Version* (NKJV), which we are using primarily in this study. A paraphrase includes the work and interpretation of only one scholar. A good paraphrase Bible can be helpful for occasional devotional reading or providing clarity to difficult passages. It often rephrases an existing translation rather than a creating a new translation from the original languages (e.g. *The Right Word*, Zondervan).

One popular paraphrase is *The Message Bible* in which the translator, Eugene H. Peterson, puts scripture into modern-day language with the help of consultants. In addition to other sources, he utilized Greek manuscripts. Our study provides a good opportunity for you to discover the way different translations or paraphrases of the Bible can enhance your study.

Returning to verse 2, let's take a look at Eugene Peterson's paraphrase of Psalm 32:2: "Count yourself lucky—God holds nothing against you and you're holding nothing back from him." Compare that to the NKJV text. Does *The Message Bible* clarify this statement, using verbiage that is easier to understand?

3. Perhaps when you read verse 8—"I will instruct you and teach you in the way you should go; I will guide you with My eye"—you did not fully comprehend how God guides someone with His eye. Write in the space below what you think this verse means.

_____
_____
_____
_____
_____
_____
_____
_____

Let's reference *The Amplified Bible*, a word-for-word translation based on the work of 13 scholars. This popular version seeks to break through the language barrier by including additional amplification of word meanings. Look at the *The Amplified Bible* translation of verse 8 and see how it compares with what you wrote above.

When you share your heart with someone and they do not look you in the eye, it makes you wonder if they are even listening. Perhaps we do the same when someone speaks to us. Does it give you joy to know that when you seek God's help, He does not take His eye off you? Let's use another tool to further understand this concept: cross-referencing.

LESSON FIVE

4. Read Genesis 16. This passage includes the first usage of one of God's names, *El Roi*, the God who sees. As you read, ask the helping questions and list below what you learn about Hagar.

   _____

   _____

   _____

   _____

   _____

   - What did Hagar learn about God through her experiences?

   _____

   _____

   _____

   _____

5. How does God's name, *El Roi*, enhance your understanding of Psalm 32:8? What did you learn about His character that can help you in your own walk with Him?

   _____

   _____

   _____

   _____

   _____

6. As mentioned earlier, some scholars refer to Psalm 32 as a "Maskil," or a poem intended for meditation. In your repeated Bible readings, you have spent time in meditation and contemplation as you carefully observed the text. Now let us see how *Strong's* defines *Maskil*.

- *Maskil* – maskîyl, *mas-keel*; …instructive, i.e. a didactic poem:—Maschil (*Strong's* 4905) *Maskil* derives from the Hebrew word *sakal*.

- *Sâkal*: *saw-kal*; a primitive root; to be (caus. make or act) circumspect and hence intelligent:— consider, expert, instruct, prosper, (deal) prudent(-ly), (give) skill (-ful), have good success, teach, (have, make to) understand(-ing), wisdom, (be, behave self, consider, make) wise (-ly), guide wittingly. (*Strong's* 7919)

Notice that this Maskil is identified as a didactic, or instructive, poem. *Strong's* uses words like *circumspect*, *teach*, *understand*, *wisdom*, and *guide* to describe the nature of this contemplative poem. In Psalm 32, David employs the term *Selah* to encourage reflection. It is with good reason that Psalm 119 repeatedly speaks of meditating on God's Word. It is often through meditation that we come to understand God's character and the benefits that He heaps upon us because He loves us. Not only that, we also learn His requirements for us so that we can live life abundantly and joyfully.

My Interpretation

Now it is time to think through what you have learned from your study of Psalm 32. You have pondered questions and answers and considered what Bible scholars have to say. As concisely as possible, write down your conclusions about the purpose of this contemplative, instructive poem and David's motivations for writing it. Wait until the Devote and Disciple sections to express what it means to you personally.

_____

_____

_____

_____

_____

_____

_____

_____

_____

_____

DEVOTE

Does joy seem elusive to you? If you are forgiven, you have every reason to experience every blessing that salvation brings—including joy. Rather than an emotion that can be worked up, joy is a gift that proceeds from the character of God. No matter the circumstances, His eye is on you and you are surrounded with songs of deliverance!

Psalm 32—God's Forgiveness is Joy Forevermore

Take time now to wait upon the Lord as you search your heart. El Roi is with you. The God who sees already knows the deep things of your heart. Speak or sing the following words from Psalm 103, a hymn written by David.

> ¹ *Bless the LORD, O my soul; And all that is within me, bless His holy name!* ² *Bless the LORD, O my soul, And forget not all His benefits:* ³ *Who forgives all your iniquities, Who heals all your diseases,* ⁴ *Who redeems your life from destruction, Who crowns you with lovingkindness and tender mercies,* ⁵ *Who satisfies your mouth with good things, So that your youth is renewed like the eagle's.*

What emotions do these words evoke in your spirit? Record them below and specify why they come to mind.

Emotion	Reason

Pause for Prayer

How sweet are Your words to my taste, Sweeter than honey to my mouth! Through Your precepts I get understanding; Therefore I hate every false way (Psalm 119:103, 104).

David's contemplation in Psalm 32:3, 4 reveals how miserable he felt after he had sinned. Before he confessed his sin, he felt physically ill, causing him to groan all day long. Perhaps it was an inward groaning that welled up in his spirit out of guilt and self-condemnation. His energy vanished as he encountered a season of emotional drought. He knew God's precepts and he knew he had disobeyed them. Instead of sweetness, the LORD's precepts tasted bitter.

Notice the change that repentance brought to his state of mind. By the last verse, David felt a release of joy because he was forgiven and among the righteous.

As you prepare your heart to put what you have learned from Psalm 32 into practice, ask yourself, "Is there anything keeping me from experiencing the fullness of joy that comes from trusting the Lord?" Compose a prayer below, asking God for understanding through His Word.

_____

_____

_____

_____

_____

DISCIPLE

Do you want to be effective as a follower of Christ in every part of your life—at home, at work, at church, in the community, among your neighbors? Of course you do! That is why you are a student of God's Word.

Is anything holding you back from fully experiencing God and living joyfully before others? Do you battle low self-esteem, ungratefulness, negativity, or unconfessed sin? His presence is with you now. His eye is on you. So ask El Roi, the God who sees, to examine your heart and guide you out of that mindset. Dwell on His character and all the benefits available to you as His child.

Let's practice contemplative praise. On a separate sheet of paper, write out 50 thank-yous to the Lord. Think about the many ways He has blessed you. Has he protected you? Has He shown you mercy? Has He demonstrated His love? When you finish your list, follow the psalmist's example and pause (*Selah*) to reflect on all the Lord has done for you.

In two or three sentences, record the ways you feel changed after taking time to concentrate on 50 blessings from God.

_____

_____

_____

Lesson Five

Now "be glad in the LORD and rejoice… shout for joy" (Psalm 32:11). In the next lesson, you will be invited to "taste and see that the LORD is good" (Psalm 34:8).

Lesson Six

Thanksgiving

A Path to Praise

Taste and See that the Lord Is Good (Psalm 34)

LESSON SIX

PSALM 34:1-22

TASTE AND SEE THAT THE LORD IS GOOD

Key Verse

Oh, magnify the LORD with me, And let us exalt His name together (Psalm 34:3).

Introduction

Have you ever felt afraid of or trapped by an authority figure? Maybe you silently asked God for wisdom, making these words from Psalm 46 your prayer: "God is [my] refuge and strength, A very present help in trouble" (v. 1). Did you sense the quiet assurance that God was in control?

David found himself in precarious circumstances when he ran for his life from King Saul and encountered Abimelech. David would not forget this experience, and he recorded it in the annals of the psalms to remind the nation of Israel of God's "very present help in trouble." Let's not get ahead of ourselves. We have some preliminary work to do before we investigate the ultimate, enduring effect of Psalm 34.

Your Exploration of the Text

Pause for Prayer

Uphold me according to Your word, that I may live; And do not let me be ashamed of my hope. Hold me up, and I shall be safe, And I shall observe Your statutes continually (Psalm 119:116-117).

You can look back on this lesson time and time again when you face trouble. The psalm's title hints at the distress that prompted David to write it. His message is clear: He sought God, God heard him, and God delivered him—in quite an unexpected way.

You may be facing trouble or fear as you begin this lesson. Before going any farther, lay it on the altar. Harness your mind and focus on God's Word. Concentrate for a few moments on the 50 thank-yous you expressed to the Lord in Lesson Five. Let them serve as a reminder of God's blessings in your life, and honor Him with a heart of gratitude. Then ask Him to lead you into all truth. Trust Him to teach you lessons for life from His Word by the power of the Holy Spirit.

THE TEXT

Psalm 34:1-22

A Psalm of David when he pretended madness before Abimelech, who drove him away, and he departed.

1 I will bless the LORD at all times; His praise shall continually be in my mouth. ² My soul shall make its boast in the LORD; The humble shall hear of it and be glad. ³ Oh, magnify the LORD with me, And let us exalt His name together. ⁴ I sought the LORD, and He heard me, And delivered me from all my fears.

⁵They looked to Him and were radiant, And their faces were not ashamed. ⁶ This poor man cried out, and the LORD heard him, And saved him out of all his troubles. ⁷ The angel of the LORD encamps all around those who fear Him, And delivers them. ⁸ Oh, taste and see that the LORD is good; Blessed is the man who

trusts in Him! ⁹ Oh, fear the LORD, you His saints! There is no want to those who fear Him. ¹⁰ The young lions lack and suffer hunger; But those who seek the LORD shall not lack any good thing. ¹¹ Come, you children, listen to me; I will teach you the fear of the LORD. ¹² Who is the man who desires life, And loves many days, that he may see good? ¹³ Keep your tongue from evil, And your lips from speaking deceit. ¹⁴ Depart from evil and do good; Seek peace and pursue it. ¹⁵ The eyes of the LORD are on the righteous, And His ears are open to their cry. ¹⁶ The face of the LORD is against those who do evil, To cut off the remembrance of them from the earth. ¹⁷ The righteous cry out, and the LORD hears, And delivers them out of all their troubles. ¹⁸ The LORD is near to those who have a broken heart, And saves such as have a contrite spirit. ¹⁹ Many are the afflictions of the righteous, But the LORD delivers him out of them all.

²⁰ He guards all his bones; Not one of them is broken. ²¹ Evil shall slay the wicked, And those who hate

Psalm 34—Taste and See that the Lord is Good

the righteous shall be condemned. ²² The LORD redeems the soul of His servants, And none of those who trust in Him shall be condemned.

DISCOVER

According to its title, Psalm 34 looks back on a specific historical event. We will learn about that time in David's life as we move through this lesson, but now it is time to saturate yourself in the living Word.

1. Quietly read Psalm 34, and meditatively keep in mind the helping questions: Who? What? Why? When? Where? How?

2. Read the passage again, intentionally focusing on the connection of the verses with one another. Do you notice a flow of thoughts as you move through the psalm?

3. Read the text aloud and write down obvious helping questions and your preliminary answers.

My Helping Questions and Answers

_____
_____
_____

Summary. Briefly summarize your observations below.

My Findings

Psalm 34—Taste and See that the Lord is Good

Every Text Has a Context

1. Identify the author of this psalm.

2. You learned in Lesson One that David authored 13 psalms that reveal historical occasions in their titles. From the title alone, what historical event inspired David to write Psalm 34?

LESSON SIX

DISCERN

Key Words Open the Door to Understanding

Read Psalm 34 several times, writing down important key words and phrases below as you go. Repetition indicates a word or phrase's importance and relevance. Add the key words and phrases to your list and mark them in the Scripture text with the colors and/or icons of your choice. Remember to transfer words from your previous key word lists.

_____
_____
_____
_____
_____
_____

1. According to your key word search, to whom does David give prominence? How many times does he mention that prominent figure?

   _____
   _____
   _____
   _____
   _____

2. Who expresses his intent to praise and then follows it with a report of deliverance? How many times are personal pronouns (I, me, etc.) used?

3. Identify the group of people mentioned often in verses 7-22? Note the various words and phrases that refer to that group of people, including pronouns. If you did not pick up on this when you were locating key words, mark all of those descriptive words and phrases the same way and record them on your key word list. David directed much of his psalm to this group. Record how many times the group is referenced in different forms.

4. In Lesson Five, you studied the word *blessed* in Psalm 32 using *The New Strong's Exhaustive Concordance of the Bible*. The same word is found in Psalm 34:8. Notice that *bless* is used in

Lesson Six

verse 1, but we will discover when we open our tool box that the meaning here is different from *blessed* in verse 8.

You may not have identified *bless* in verse 1 as a key word because it appears only once. However, several other words with similar meanings are sprinkled throughout the first few verses of the chapter. Find those words and record them below. Add them to your key word list, and then mark them in the text along with *bless*—perhaps with a green megaphone.

5. Mark time references in the text and record them below. They emphasize the importance David places on praising the LORD.

PSALM 34—TASTE AND SEE THAT THE LORD IS GOOD   151

6. As you were uncovering key words, you certainly observed that *praise* and its synonyms were the essence of verses 1-3. In the chart below, divide each verse into two parts.

Verse	Part One	Part Two
1		
2		
3		

David moves from praising God to recounting all He has done. Continue your chart below with verses 4-6.

Verse	Part One	Part Two
4		
5		
6		

Earlier, you identified a group of people that David mentioned repeatedly in verses 7-22. Did you recognize David's words here as an exhortation to those people? He used the same pattern in verses 7-22 that he utilized in verses 1-6. Continue your chart below.

Verse	Part One	Part Two
7		

Lesson Six

Verse	Part One	Part Two
8		
9		
10		
11		
12		
13		
14		
15		
16		
17		
18		
19		
20		
21		
22		

Are you beginning to sense the poetic structure of Psalm 34? We will cover this idea later in the study.

Psalm 34—Taste and See that the Lord is Good

Compile Lists

Your key word study showed that David used a variety of words and phrases to describe a group of people. Did you recognize them as the righteous? His emphasis on the righteous is reflected in the number of times he mentions them—at least 24 times.

Review Psalm 34 verse by verse. List below each name assigned to the righteous in the left column and the benefits bestowed on them in the right column. Rather than writing the entire verse, just summarize. We have included some examples to get you started.

Verse	Name Assigned by David to the Righteous	Benefits Bestowed on the Righteous
7	Those who fear Him	Angel of the LORD encamps all around them He delivers them
8	The man who trusts in Him	Blessed
9	His saints	No want
10		
11		
12		
13		
14		
15		

Lesson Six

16		
17		
18		
19		
20		
21		
22		

Contrast Makes the Difference

1. Remember, we contrast words or phrases to compare opposite ideas, individuals, and/or items. When you discover contrasts in the text, put a bracket to the left of the verse(s) and write "contrast." Keep in mind that the words *but*, *however*, or *nevertheless* may be clues that two different things are being compared. When you find such a word, underline it and record what you discover in the space below, along with the scripture reference.

_____

_____

_____

_____

_____

2. Verse 14 might be mistaken for a contrast because of the difference between *good* and *evil*. However, there is no indication that anything is being compared. If the verse read, "The wicked practice evil, *but* the righteous do good," that would be a contrast between the wicked and the righteous, but that is not the case.

3. You've established that there are many benefits attributed to the righteous in Psalm 34, but now look for another group of people (let's call them "the unrighteous") and record the consequences of their actions below.

Verse	Consequences of Unrighteous Actions

Build on What You Have Learned

Recall that you are learning "precept upon precept… line upon line, Here a little, there a little" (Isaiah 28:13). With that in mind, do you see a reference to the LORD in Psalm 34 which evokes one of His names that we studied in a previous lesson? Write the name below and include the reference from Psalm 34.

_____

_____

_____

_____

_____

_____

_____

_____

You are weaving a thread of understanding through Scripture by the discipline of studying God's Word inductively. Make a note of the Genesis 16 cross-reference alongside Psalm 34:15 in your Bible. This will be a useful reminder in your future Bible studies.

Pause for Prayer

My tongue shall speak of Your word, For all Your commandments are righteousness. Let Your hand become my help, For I have chosen Your precepts (Psalm 119:172-173).

If you have accepted Jesus Christ as your Lord and Savior, your sins have been forgiven and you have chosen to follow His precepts. You stand in the right place—a place of commitment to learn and obey His Word. The joy of the Lord has become your strength and you can sing of His Word.

As you pause for prayer, meditate for a moment on the Israelites' dilemma when they returned to Jerusalem after being in Babylonian captivity. Under Nehemiah's supervision, they had rebuilt the broken-down walls of the city, but homes had not been rebuilt and few people lived within those walls. The Israelites had gathered from surrounding cities to celebrate the Feast of Tabernacles and the people listened as Ezra read from the Book of the Law (see Nehemiah 8). The Scripture strongly affected the listeners: They wept at the words of the Law, raising their hands, bowing their heads, and worshipping the LORD.

Nehemiah comforted them by saying, "Do not sorrow, for the joy of the LORD is your strength" (v. 10). They went on their way to eat, drink, and rejoice greatly, for they understood the words that were declared to them.

The challenge as you continue expanding on what you have learned is to have joy in the journey. If you have found some of the assignments lengthy or cumbersome, tell that to the Lord. Let Him know that you choose to be diligent in studying His Word because you want to know Him. Ask Him to put a song of joy in your heart. David's heart's cry can be yours as well. Through the power of the Holy Spirit who dwells in you, take up that cry and praise the Lord for the benefits that are yours simply because you belong to Him.

Pulling It All Together

Cross-Referencing

1. The title assigned to Psalm 34 tells us that it proceeded from a time in David's life when he "pretended madness before Abimelech." Read 1 Samuel 19—21 to understand David's predicament when he fled from King Saul, who sought to kill him out of jealousy. The account of David seeking refuge from to Achish (also known as Abimelech), the king of Gath, reveals

Lesson Six

David's fear and erratic behavior. Write a brief synopsis of chapters 20 and 21.

_____
_____
_____
_____
_____
_____

- Although David did not address his specific experience with Abimelech in Psalm 34, it obviously was etched in his memory. That unforgettable episode prompted him to express his gratitude for God's deliverance.

2. Now that you are familiar with the historical occasion that inspired Psalm 34, identify the specific elements of this thanksgiving psalm. The characteristics appear in a different configuration than we have seen before. Record the verse references in the column provided.

Element	Verse Locations
Intent to Praise	
Report of Deliverance	
Exhortation to Wisdom	

3. Notice that David shares the lessons he learned from his own experience without revealing the details of that event. By leaving out the specifics, David allows readers to insert their own

circumstances. Think of a crisis you have experienced, record it below, and explain how God delivered you out of trouble.

_____
_____
_____
_____
_____
_____
_____

4. All Christians have experienced God's deliverance. You can join with the multitudes who sing, "Oh, magnify the LORD with me, And let us exalt His name together" (Psalms 34:3). Draw a box around this key verse in the text.

Open Your Tool Box

1. In Lesson Five, you learned that one meaning of *blessed* is "happiness; how happy!" Another meaning is "consecrated, sanctified, set apart." The same word used in Psalm 32:1,2 appears in Psalm 34:8. Let's research the word bless in *The New Strong's Exhaustive Concordance of the Bible*.

   - *Bless*: barak *baw-rak*; a primitive root; to kneel; by implication to bless God (as an act of adoration)… kneel (down), praise, salute; …thank. (*Strong's* 1288)

If you studied other similar words found in the text, you would discover that the Hebrew definitions of *praise*, *boast*, *magnify*, and *exalt* have similar meaning with varying nuances. You marked them all in the same way for that reason.

2. In Lessons Four and Five, you were introduced to a royal psalm and a Maskil, or contemplation. David wrote Psalm 34 as an alphabetic acrostic. Each line or stanza of the poem begins with a letter of the Hebrew alphabet in order. Acrostics serve to aid the memory. Since the Hebrew alphabet has 22 letters, there are 22 lines in the poem. Now that you understand the thought behind these lyrics, do you have a greater appreciation for David's effort?

3. One of your helping questions may have been, "Whose faces were radiant in verse 5, and whose faces were not ashamed?" Now that you have completed discovering and discerning on your own, go to outside resources for further clarification.

One source could be a different version of the Bible, such as the *New International Version*, which translates verse 5, "Those who look to him are radiant; their faces are never covered with shame." That provides some clarity, but to whom do the words refer?

A reputable, conservative commentary could serve as another valuable resource. *The Pulpit Commentary* (William B. Eerdman's Publishing Company, Grand Rapids, Michigan) gives an explanation that may shed light on the report of deliverance.

Psalm 34—Taste and See that the Lord is Good

First the psalmist speaks for himself (verse 4). But what is true of one is true of many. Let each of us put himself in "this poor man's" place. Recall the peril and the prayer…the gracious deliverance…God's deliverance brings gladness…We see in them the outshining of his love…

While it is best to discover all you can on your own, along with the help of the Holy Spirit, there is value in turning to biblical scholars for guidance.

4. Think about what you just read. Considering that Psalm 34:7-22 serves as an exhortation, how does David draw his audience into this poem? Record below how he does this and briefly explain your conclusions.

_____
_____
_____
_____
_____
_____
_____
_____

My Interpretation

Express in your own words how you think this acrostic poem spoke to the nation of Israel over 3,000 years ago.

LESSON SIX

_____

DEVOTE

In Lesson Five, you meditated on God's blessings in your life by reflecting on His goodness and mercy and listing 50 thank-yous. This lesson speaks of the psalmist blessing God—praising Him, boasting in Him, magnifying Him, and exalting Him. Make a list of 50 praises, focusing on God's character rather than His specific gifts to you. Praying through Psalm 34 will get you started. Add to your list as you dwell on and praise God for who He is.

Your two lists provide two perspectives on God's role in your life: His everyday blessings awaken our gratitude and His holy attributes inspire our praise. Compare the two lists and make any observations.

Pause for Prayer

I have chosen the way of truth; Your judgments I have laid before me. I cling to Your testimonies; O LORD, do not put me to shame! I will run the course of Your commandments, For You shall enlarge my heart (Psalm 119:30-32).

David experienced a wide range of emotions that quickened his spirit to write this thought-provoking poem. It stood as a memorial for him, an exhortation for the nation of Israel, and a message for God's people down through the ages—including us.

Are you seeking deliverance from unresolved problems, lingering grievances, strained relationships, or some self-inflicted difficulty? Do you want to receive "beauty for ashes, The oil of joy for mourning, The garment of praise for the spirit of heaviness" (Isaiah 61:3)? Perhaps you long to know the Lord in a deeper way so that you may be called a tree of righteousness, "The planting of the LORD, that He may be glorified." Begin by turning your face to the Lord and blessing Him. Boast in Him. Magnify the Lord with the saints of all the ages. Exalt His name. Look to Him and be radiant! Look to Him and do not be ashamed! Enjoy a time of refreshing right here, right now. Meditate and pray through Psalm 34:1-6, recording any thoughts below.

_____
_____
_____
_____
_____
_____
_____
_____

DISCIPLE

Psalm 34 overflows with exhortations to the righteous. You listed them in the Discern section. You found incitements, commands, and promises for those who trust in the Lord. Although God inspired David to write this poem 3,000 years ago, it is also for you. That should give you pause—Selah. Examine your heart as you contemplate verses 7-22. Ask the Holy Spirit to quicken your spirit to see any changes you need to make. Then ask God to help you to motivate others through a life lived only for the glory of God. Memorialize your thoughts and prayers in the space provided.

_____
_____
_____
_____
_____
_____
_____

Have you tasted the goodness of the Lord through this lesson? Lift your radiant face toward Him and "magnify the Lord with me, And let us exalt His name together" (Psalm 34:3).

In Lesson Seven, you will continue searching God's Word with a heart of thanks and praise. Discovering Him as *El Elyon*, the Most High, will fill you with awe and delight.

Lesson Seven

Thanksgiving

A Path to Praise

It is Good to Give Thanks to the Lord (Psalm 92)

LESSON SEVEN

PSALM 92:1-15

IT IS GOOD TO GIVE THANKS TO THE LORD

Key Verse

It is good to give thanks to the LORD, And to sing praises to Your name, O Most High (Psalm 92:1).

Introduction

You concluded Lesson Six by giving thanks to the LORD, singing praises to His name, and meditating on His character. The best way to praise Him is to live your life according to His will. How can you know His will? By continuing what you are doing—diligently studying His Word under the guidance of the Holy Spirit. Another way is to live each day, from morning to night, with an attitude of prayer. Follow Paul's teachings in 1 Thessalonians 5:16-18: "Rejoice always, pray without ceasing, in everything give thanks." Keep in touch with God by praying with joy and thanksgiving. As you navigate your way through

Psalm 92, you will see the power this kind of communion brings.

Your Exploration of the Text

Pause for Prayer

Your statutes have been my songs In the house of my pilgrimage. I remember Your name in the night, O LORD, And I keep Your law (Psalm 119:54-55).

How often have you laid your head on your pillow at night singing praise to the Lord for His goodness and mercy? On the other hand, how often have you cried out the Lord's name in the night, asking Him to show you His goodness and mercy in the middle of a trial? Pause for a few moments right now to tell Him what is on your heart. You may boldly say, "The LORD is on my side; I will not fear. What can man do to me?" (Psalm 118:6). He has promised to "never leave you nor forsake you" (Hebrews 13:5), so enter into His presence. Give Him praise and confess your fears. Ask Him to use this study of Psalm 92 to reveal Himself to you in a fresh way.

Psalm 92—It is Good to Give Thanks to the Lord

THE TEXT

PSALM 92:1-15

A Psalm. A Song for the Sabbath day.

¹ It is good to give thanks to the LORD, And to sing praises to Your name, O Most High; ² To declare Your lovingkindness in the morning, And Your faithfulness every night, ³ On an instrument of ten strings, On the lute, And on the harp, With harmonious sound. ⁴ For You, LORD, have made me glad through Your work; I will triumph in the works of Your hands. ⁵ O LORD, how great are Your works! Your thoughts are very deep. ⁶ A senseless man does not know, Nor does a fool understand this. ⁷ When the wicked spring up like grass, And when all the workers of iniquity flourish, It is that they may be destroyed forever. ⁸ But You, LORD, are on high forevermore. ⁹ For behold, Your enemies, O

LORD, For behold, Your enemies shall perish; All the workers of iniquity shall be scattered. ¹⁰ But my horn You have exalted like a wild ox; I have been anointed with fresh oil. ¹¹ My eye also has seen my desire on my enemies; My ears hear my desire on the wicked Who rise up against me. ¹² The righteous shall flourish like a palm tree, He shall grow like a cedar in Lebanon.¹³ Those who are planted in the house of the LORD Shall flourish in the courts of our God. ¹⁴ They shall still bear fruit in old age; They shall be fresh and flourishing, ¹⁵ To declare that the LORD is upright; He is my rock, and there is no unrighteousness in Him.

DISCOVER

Meditating prayerfully on this psalm allows you to step back into time and embrace an important part of Jewish history.

Psalm 92—It is Good to Give Thanks to the Lord

1. Beginning with the title, read this psalm line by line. By now, it will be natural for you to mentally ask the helping questions. Do not dwell on those questions at this time.

2. Read the passage again, focusing on the writer's thoughts and emotions. What do you feel as you absorb the text?

   _____
   _____
   _____
   _____
   _____

3. Now read Psalm 92 aloud. Think intentionally about the helping questions, and write your answers below.

My Helping Questions and Answers

_____
_____
_____
_____
_____
_____
_____

Lesson Seven

Summary. Briefly summarize your observations below.

My Findings

___

___

___

___

___

___

___

___

___

___

___

___

Every Text Has a Context

1. Do we know who authored this psalm?

   ___

   ___

2. According to the title, for what purpose was this psalm used?

_____

_____

_____

_____

_____

DISCERN

Key Words Open the Door to Understanding

It would be wonderful to step back in time and join in Sabbath worship with the Israelites, led by a Chief Musician. Imagine singing with the Levites, accompanied by cymbals, strings, and harps. You will get a glimpse of that experience as you study Psalm 92.

This song was written by an unknown psalmist specifically for use on the Sabbath day. Let's use our inductive study tools to discover its central message.

Begin by making a key word list. As you read through the chapter several times, find repeated words and phrases and write them on your growing list and mark them in the text with the colors and/or icons of your choice. Remember to transfer words from your previous key word lists.

LESSON SEVEN

Interpreting the Meaning

1. Whom is the object of the psalmist's focus? Count the number of references.

2. You marked several related words that introduced a worshipful atmosphere in verses 1 and 2 and concluded the worship in verse 15. Write those words below.

3. How does the psalmist draw his audience into the spirit of worship?

4. Given that this is a thanksgiving psalm, how does the psalmist accomplish his purpose of invoking praise at both the opening and closing of the psalm?

5. Did you notice the variety of musical references? Mark all the words and phrases related to music, perhaps with a purple musical note. Write the references.

LESSON SEVEN

6. Psalm 92 includes several references to time. Some are subtle, while others are more obvious. Such words as *until*, *when*, *then*, and *after this*, are clues to timing or sequence of events. Time may also be expressed in stages of life. Record your discoveries by marking time references in the text. Write time-related words or phrases below.

_____

_____

_____

_____

_____

_____

7. Terms of conclusion connect the text with its expected outcome. These include words like *therefore*, *for this reason*, *for*, and *so that*. One such term appears in verse 4. Note the statement, the term of conclusion, and the result below.

_____

_____

_____

_____

_____

_____

_____

Psalm 92—It is Good to Give Thanks to the Lord

Begin at verse 1 and record each mention of God's character traits in the chart below. Focus only on the LORD's identity and attributes, as expressed in these verses.

Verse	God's Character

Note these characteristics of God in the margin of your Bible, creating a thread for easy reference.

In verse 6, the psalmist introduces a person who knows nothing of God as He is described in the previous lines. How does the psalmist define this person?

_____

_____

_____

_____

_____

Complete the chart below to show the characteristics and behavioral consequences of the senseless man. When you marked your key words, did you identify all of the words that relate to this man

Lesson Seven

(*senseless*, *fool*, *wicked*, *iniquity*, *enemies*)? If not, do so now, and record them in the text, perhaps with a squiggly brown oval around each word.

Verse	Characteristics of the Senseless Man	Behavorial Consequences of the Senseless Man

Contrast Makes the Difference

Now you will discover how vastly different the senseless fool is from the LORD and His people. As you continue to observe the text, look for words or phrases that show this contrast. Remember, the words *but*, *however*, or *nevertheless* often signify contrast. When you see such a word, underline it. When you discover the contrast(s), put a bracket to the left of the verse(s) and write "contrast." Record what you discover in the space below.

Verse	Contrast	Connecting Word	Contrast
7-8			
7-8 12-14			

PSALM 92—IT IS GOOD TO GIVE THANKS TO THE LORD   181

9　10			

    Did you notice how the psalmist uses personal pronouns in verses 10, 11, and 15 and third-person pronouns in verses 12-14? Think about the experience of congregational worship and consider how this may have influenced his terminology. Do not think in terms of a right or wrong answer. Simply express the psalmist's reasoning as you see it.

_____
_____
_____
_____
_____
_____
_____
_____

Look for Words of Comparison

1. As you were reading, you probably noticed words of comparison. While words of *contrast* show how things are opposites, words of *comparison* show how things are alike. Signals of comparison

182 Lesson Seven

include *like* or *as*. Read Psalm 92 again and look for comparison words. Connect them with a bracket in the text.

2. Complete the chart below.

Verse	Subject and Verb	Term of Comparison	The Analogy
7			
10			
12			
12			

This exercise should have given you a mental picture of the difference between the stability of the wicked and the righteous? Now use your colored pencils to illustrate the analogy that corresponds with each subject and verb. Feel free to draw as simply, or as creatively, as you wish.

Psalm 92—It is Good to Give Thanks to the Lord

The wicked spring up like grass	
My horn You have exalted like a wild ox	
The righteous shall flourish like a palm tree	
He shall grow like a cedar in Lebanon	

Pause for Prayer

I will never forget Your precepts, For by them You have given me life (Psalm 119:93).

If you have surrendered your life to Jesus Christ and believed in Him—that He died for your sins, was buried, and rose on the third day—then you have been declared *righteous*. *The Amplified Bible* says it well in Romans 5:1, "Therefore, since we are justified (acquitted, declared righteous, and given a right standing with God) through faith, let us [grasp the fact that we] have [the peace of reconciliation to hold and to enjoy] peace with God through our Lord Jesus Christ (the Messiah, the Anointed One)." Second Corinthians 5:21 states, "For He made Him who knew no sin to be sin for us, that we might become the righteousness of God in Him." As a believer, your life has been renewed. The Lord continues to renew your life day by day through the power of the Holy Spirit, quickening His Word in your spirit.

Because of your right standing with God, all of the benefits of the righteous as declared in Psalm 92 belong to you. Take a few moments now to praise God for your identity in Him. Your contrast and comparison charts and your drawings reveal all He has designed you to be. Review them and spend some time in prayer.

Pulling It All Together

Core focus and major themes

By now, you know that the various elements of the thanksgiving psalms, including Psalm 92, are revealed in a variety of ways. List the references for each element below.

Psalm 92—It is Good to Give Thanks to the Lord

Element	Verse Locations
Intent to Praise	
Report of Deliverance	
Renewed Vow to Praise	

Open Your Tool Box

Now that you have searched the text and come to many conclusions for yourself, you will look to outside sources for further insight.

1. Psalm 92 is the only "Sabbath" psalm in the Book of Psalms. It would have been sung during weekly worship.

2. Understanding the names of God that are revealed in Scripture adds to our depth of knowledge and worship of Him. Notice in verse 1 that the psalmist sings praises to God's name, *Most High*. We will return to *Strong's* for details from the original Hebrew text.

    - *Most High*: 'elyôwn, *el-yone'*… an elevation i.e. lofty; as title, the Supreme: (Most, on) high (-er, -est), upper (-most). (*Strong's*, 5945)

Lesson Seven

You have probably seen God's name "Most High" expressed as *El Elyon*. Based on *Strong's* definition, describe the Most High God in your own words.

_____
_____
_____
_____
_____
_____
_____

3. Read Genesis 14:18-20 to discover where "God Most High" first appears in Scripture. Pay special attention to the way Melchizedek defines God. List God's mighty acts as expressed in Melchizedek's prayer.

_____
_____
_____
_____

4. Read Daniel 4:34, 35. How does King Nebuchadnezzar define the supremacy of the Most High?

_____
_____
_____
_____

Psalm 92—It is Good to Give Thanks to the Lord

Knowing that the God you serve reigns supreme as the sovereign ruler of the universe should give you pause. *Selah.* Consider the depth with which the psalmist praises God in this Sabbath song.

5. In verses 4 and 5, the psalmist expounds on God's sovereignty by proclaiming the greatness of His works. Beth Tanner offers a short explanation of God's works in *The Old Testament International Commentary on the Old Testament, The Book of Psalms.*

   - Verses 4 and 5 give reasons for praise. The first two words, *deeds* (v. 4) and *work* (v. 5), encompass both God's saving acts (Deut. 32:4; Isa. 45:11; Exod. 34:10; Josh. 24:31) and God's creative acts (Ps. 8:6; 19:1) (p. 704).

   - Read the scriptures referenced above and list God's saving acts and creative acts below. Consider the context of each scripture in your research.

Scripture	Saving Acts	Creative Acts
Deuteronomy 32:4		
Isaiah 45:11-13		
Exodus 34:10		

Lesson Seven

Joshua 24:31		
Psalm 8:6		
Psalm 19:1		

6. For further clarification on verse 11, we will utilize the New International Version (NIV) of the Bible. Compare the NKJV to the NIV below:

NKJV	NIV
My eye also has seen my desire on my enemies: My ears hear my desire on the wicked Who rise up against me.	My eyes have seen the defeat of my adversaries; my ears have heard the rout of my wicked foes.

Can you envision the deliverance that the psalmist and the singers have experienced—or perhaps anticipate in faith? Picture enemies being routed, defeated, and dispersed.

7. The psalmists employed various literary devices to convey their messages. In Psalm 32, David expressed his contemplative mood in the form of a Maskil. In Psalm 34, he composed an alphabetic acrostic.

Psalm 92—It is Good to Give Thanks to the Lord

The author of Psalm 92 uses a technique identified by scholars as *climactic parallelism*. Refer to verses 7, 9, and 11, noting that each verse is composed of three lines. On the chart, copy each line in the applicable column.

Verse	A-line	B-line	Added Phrase
7			
9			
11			

Parallelism—or balanced repetition—forms the foundation of Hebrew poetry. The cadence of the Psalms, even in translation, rises mainly from various types of parallelism. Usually two parallel lines appear together, forming a "bicolon" or a "distich." In Psalm 92, however, three parallel lines are utilized, creating a "tricolon" or a "tristich." The result is a highly repetitive, slowly advancing set of lines [www.biblegateway.com]. This construction is called *climactic parallelism*. Notice on your chart that the B-line echoes part of the A-line, then a third phrase is added that develops the meaning and completes the sentence [www.westminster.edu].

Read each verse aloud and notice the poetic cadence. Do you sense the momentum building in the first two lines and then culminating in the third line?

Summary. Spend a little time interpreting Psalm 92 in your own words.

My Interpretation

_____
_____
_____
_____
_____
_____
_____
_____
_____

DEVOTE

How does the knowledge you have gained from this lesson affect your attitude toward personal and corporate worship? Do you stand in awe of the sovereign ruler of the universe despite seeing "the wicked spring up like grass" and "all the workers of iniquity flourish"? Are you humbled by God's promises to His righteous ones, both ancient and modern? How does this knowledge deepen your devotion to *El Elyon*, God Most High?

Why should we "rejoice always, pray without ceasing, in everything give thanks" (1 Thessalonians 5:16-18) and worship God with joy and thanksgiving? Did you uncover the answers in your study of Psalm 92? Record your conclusions below.

_____
_____
_____
_____
_____
_____
_____
_____
_____
_____

Try your hand at writing a song, as short or as long as you like, expressing your thoughts from Psalm 92. If you have musical skills, put your words to a melody. The following lyrics are the writer's expression:

Oh, Your lovingkindness
Oh, yes, Your faithfulness
Wake me in the morning
Put me to bed at night

You're my sure foundation
You are my solid Rock
On high forevermore
Most High forevermore

Now it is your turn. Write your lyrics below.

_____
_____
_____
_____
_____
_____
_____

Pause for Prayer

The proud have me in great derision, Yet I do not turn aside from Your law. I remembered Your judgments of old, O LORD, And have comforted myself. Indignation has taken hold of me Because of the wicked, who forsake Your law (Psalm 119:51-53).

Psalm 92—It is Good to Give Thanks to the Lord

Do you encounter people at work, in your circle of friends, or perhaps in your family who are senseless or foolish? They do not recognize, much less understand, God's greatness. They do not have, or even desire, an intimate relationship with Him. They may not be your enemies, but they are not on the same page as you where God is concerned. Do you wish to convey God's sovereignty and righteousness in your sphere of influence without appearing self-righteous?

Stop right now, right here, and ask for God's wisdom. Tell Him you want to show others the lovingkindness and faithfulness He has imparted to you. Ask Him to put a song in your heart. Ask Him to exalt you like a wild ox and anoint you with fresh oil. He wants you to flourish like a palm tree and grow like a cedar in Lebanon. His desire is for you to bear fruit in old age, still fresh and flourishing. Why? Write the answer from verse 15 below.

_____

_____

_____

_____

_____

_____

_____

_____

Bow before Him now, and tell Him you want these blessings so that you can reflect His beauty and His goodness in your life, for His glory.

DISCIPLE

Take a few moments to mentally walk through a typical Sunday morning. You prepare for church, travel there, enter the sanctuary, and participate in the worship service. What emotions do entering the sanctuary and joining in worship invoke?

If you attend, or have attended, a Pentecostal church, you are certainly aware that music is an important element of worship. Do you participate in worshipful singing? Or are you distracted by things and people around you? Think about your actions and those of the song leader and congregation. Do you perceive that God Most High holds the central place?

How can you create a worshipful environment during corporate singing and the other parts of worship (prayer, collection of the offering, preaching, etc.). Write your ideas in the space provided.

_____
_____
_____
_____

Psalm 92—It is Good to Give Thanks to the Lord

_____
_____
_____

Take these thoughts with you to the next worship service you attend. Ask God to help you reign in your mind to worship Him for who He is—God Most High.

Remember that your everyday life is an act of worship toward Him. Read Romans 12:1, 2 and note God's instructions below.

_____
_____
_____
_____
_____
_____

You have successfully completed another lesson using the inductive Bible study approach. Focusing on the LORD and His character in the thanksgiving psalms will give you a fresh perspective of the living God.

Are you looking forward to studying Psalm 118? It will put a new song in your heart!

Lesson Eight

Thanksgiving

A Path to Praise

Praise God, His Mercy Endures Forever (Psalm 118)

LESSON EIGHT

PSALM 118:1-14, 29

PRAISE, GOD, HIS MERCY ENDURES FOREVER

Key Verse

Oh, give thanks to the LORD, for He is good! For His mercy endures forever (Psalm 118:1).

Introduction

Have you attended a worship service since completing Lesson Seven? If so, did you reflect on what you learned? Were you more conscious of your attitude and the One you were worshiping than your physical surroundings?

Perhaps you had a busy week and rushed to get ready for church and the responsibilities that followed. During frantic times, it is especially important to reign in your thoughts and focus on God Most High. When you are overwhelmed with the stresses of life, follow the admonition of Hebrews

13:15 in the church and in everyday life: "Therefore by Him let us continually offer the sacrifice of praise to God, that is, the fruit of our lips, giving thanks to His name."

As we discussed in the last lesson, your daily life is an act of worship toward Him. You learned from Romans 12:1-2 to "present your bodies a living sacrifice, holy, acceptable to God, which is your reasonable service. And do not be conformed to this world, but be transformed by the renewing of your mind, that you may prove what is that good and acceptable and perfect will of God." With that in mind, let's move on to Psalm 118. In this lesson, we will see how the psalmist handled distress.

Your Exploration of the Text

Pause for Prayer

You have dealt well with Your servant, O LORD, according to Your word... You are good, and do good; Teach me Your statutes (Psalm 119:65, 68).

Jesus was confronted by Satan in the wilderness after He had been fasting for 40 days and nights. He was hungry and Satan tempted Him to turn stones into bread. Jesus responded with a quote from Deuteronomy 8:3: "[M]an shall not live by bread alone; but man lives by every word that proceeds from the mouth of the LORD." Just as the heavenly Father held Jesus up in the wilderness by His Word, He holds you up and protects you when you are in distress. Jeremiah 23:29 tells us God's Word is "like a fire" and "like a hammer that breaks the rock in pieces." It is vital to know God's Word, our

PSALM 118—PRAISE GOD, HIS MERCY ENDURES FOREVER

weapon during times of stress and spiritual warfare. "[A]bove all, taking the shield of faith with which you will be able to quench all the fiery darts of the wicked one. And take the helmet of salvation, and the sword of the Spirit, which is the word of God" (Ephesians 6:16, 17).

A soldier does not engage in war without full knowledge of his or her weapon. Likewise, you must know your weapon. Your study of God's Word is essential. When the enemy surrounds you, you can be more than a conqueror through the power of the Holy Spirit and the power of the Word of God.

Begin this lesson with prayer. Your teacher, the Holy Spirit, always stands ready to guide you in the learning experience. Spend a few moments submitting to Him with anticipation and faith.

THE TEXT

Psalm 118:1-14, 29

¹ Oh, give thanks to the LORD, for He is good! For His mercy endures forever. ² Let Israel now say, "His mercy endures forever." ³ Let the house of Aaron now say, "His mercy endures forever." ⁴ Let

those who fear the LORD now say, "His mercy endures forever." [5] I called on the LORD in distress; The LORD answered me and set me in a broad place. [6] The LORD is on my side; I will not fear. What can man do to me? [7] The LORD is for me among those who help me; Therefore I shall see my desire on those who hate me. [8] It is better to trust in the LORD Than to put confidence in man. [9] It is better to trust in the LORD Than to put confidence in princes. [10] All nations surrounded me, But in the name of the LORD I will destroy them. [11] They surrounded me, Yes, they surrounded me; But in the name of the LORD I will destroy them. [12] They surrounded me like bees; They were quenched like a fire of thorns; For in the name of the LORD I will destroy them. [13] You pushed me violently, that I might fall, But the LORD helped me. [14] The LORD is my strength and song, And He has become my salvation. [15] The voice of rejoicing and salvation Is in the tents of the righteous; The right hand of the

Psalm 118—Praise God, His Mercy Endures Forever

LORD does valiantly. ¹⁶ The right hand of the LORD is exalted; The right hand of the LORD does valiantly. ¹⁷ I shall not die, but live, And declare the works of the LORD. ¹⁸ The LORD has chastened me severely, But He has not given me over to death. ¹⁹ Open to me the gates of righteousness; I will go through them, And I will praise the LORD. ²⁰ This is the gate of the LORD, Through which the righteous shall enter. ²¹ I will praise You, For You have answered me, And have become my salvation.

²² The stone which the builders rejected Has become the chief cornerstone. ²³ This was the LORD's doing; It is marvelous in our eyes. ²⁴ This is the day the LORD has made; We will rejoice and be glad in it. ²⁵ Save now, I pray, O LORD; O LORD, I pray, send now prosperity. ²⁶ Blessed is he who comes in the name of the LORD! We have blessed you from the house of the LORD. ²⁷ God is the LORD, And He has given us light; Bind the sacrifice with cords to the horns of the altar. ²⁸ You are my God,

LESSON EIGHT

and I will praise You; You are my God, I will exalt You. ²⁹ Oh, give thanks to the LORD, for He is good! For His mercy endures forever.

DISCOVER

Scholars consider Psalm 118 to be a complex psalm. While the complexity of the entire psalm is worth noting, we will narrow our focus to the verses that reveal the psalmist's personal experience and deliverance: verses 1-14 and verse 29. Go ahead and include verses 15-28 in your first reading, but we will give particular attention to verses 1-14 and 29 throughout the remainder of the lesson.

1. Begin by reading the entire psalm, paying special attention to verses 1-14 and 29.

2. Now, prayerfully read verses 1-14 and 29 a second time. Begin to absorb what the psalmist is saying.

3. Read Psalm 118:1-14, 29 aloud. Begin to organize your thoughts as you use the helping questions. Record your thoughts below.

Psalm 118—Praise God, His Mercy Endures Forever

My Helping Questions and Answers

Lesson Eight

Summary. Briefly summarize your observations below.

My Findings

Psalm 118—Praise God, His Mercy Endures Forever

Every Text Has a Context

1. What element is missing from Psalm 118 that has appeared in the other thanksgiving psalms we have studied so far?

   _____
   _____
   _____
   _____

2. Is the author identified in the text?

   _____
   _____
   _____

3. While we do not know the identity of the psalmist, we can learn some things about him from the text. To help put the text in context, review the passage again. This time, look for clues about the author and the events inspiring him to write this psalm. Record your discoveries below. Be sure to include the verse reference.

Verse	Discoveries About the Psalmist
1-4	The people are being called to worship. Therefore, the writer must have intended for the message of the psalm to be heard by the people.

208 LESSON EIGHT

DISCERN

Key Words Open the Door to Understanding

Do you find key word research helpful and enlightening? Repeated examination of the text saturates your mind with its content. Read through the chapter several times, watching for repeated words and phrases. Write them in the space provided below. Add them to your key word list and mark them in the text with the colors and/or icons of your choice. Remember to transfer words from your previous key word lists.

_____

_____

_____

_____

Psalm 118—Praise God, His Mercy Endures Forever

1. Once again, the psalmist focuses on a prominent figure. Can you identify this central character? Look at your key word markings, count the number of references, and write the number below.

   _____

   _____

   _____

   Does the task of finding the word and counting the number of times it was used help you see the value of marking the key words with specific colors or icons?

   Through your studies of the thanksgiving psalms, you have seen that the LORD is at the center of each one. You are becoming more familiar with the character of the mighty God you serve.

2. Read Psalm 118:1-14, 29 and list below the attributes and actions that reveal God's character. For example, in verse 13, one of His characteristics is "helper."

Verse	Attributes/Actions that Reveal God's Character	Verse	Attributes/Actions that Reveal God's Character

LESSON EIGHT

Take a moment to transfer these attributes and actions to the margin of your Bible.

3. You probably noticed several repeated phrases. The psalmist obviously intended to make a point through repetition. Record the repeated phrases below.

Verse	Repeated Phrase
1, 29	
1-4, 29	
8-9	
10-12	

4. Summarize the point the psalmist is making.

_____

_____

_____

_____

_____

5. Recall that a contrast expresses things that are different from one another. It may be used to introduce a rejected alternative in a contrast between two alternatives in order to state a preference.

PSALM 118—PRAISE GOD, HIS MERCY ENDURES FOREVER

The conjunction "than" may be used to introduce the contrast. You probably included the phrases in verses 8 and 9 in your repeated-phrase chart above. Identify the contrasting phrases in those two verses, and record them on the chart below.

Verse	First Alternative	Connecting Words	Rejected Alternative
8			
9			

6. In verses 10-12, the psalmist declares, "in the name of the LORD I will destroy them." Whom will he destroy?

_____

_____

_____

_____

7. A contrast can mark a significant shift in thoughts or circumstances. Note the psalmist's negative situation in each verse, the connecting word, and the positive outcome. We've used verse 10 as an example to get you started.

LESSON EIGHT

Verse	The Psalmist's Distressing Situation	Connecting Words	The Outcome
10	All nations surrounded me,	but	in the name of the Lord I will destroy them.
11			
12			
13			

8. You will find some comparisons among these verses. Comparisons include words that are alike or similar, often signified by such words as *like* or *as*. Note the comparisons below and underline the connecting words.

Verse	Comparison
12a	
12b	

9. The psalmist testified to his life-threatening experience in vivid language. If you marked the pronouns as key words in the text, you noticed that he was speaking in first-person. He shared

many ingredients for victorious living that you can apply to your own life. Divide verses 1-14 into three sections and summarize the psalmist's testimony.

Verses 1-4	Verses 5-9	Verses 10-14

10. As you have seen from your thorough reading of the text, the author speaks from his personal experience. How does he draw the worshippers into that experience?

LESSON EIGHT

Find Time

Terms of Conclusion

1. Write verses 1 and 29 below.

2. Terms of conclusion connect a verse with its outcome. These terms include *therefore*, *for this reason*, *for*, and *so that*. Did you notice a term of conclusion in verses 1 and 29? Underline each use of the term. Write the word in the space provided and explain its significance.

Psalm 118—Praise God, His Mercy Endures Forever

_____
_____
_____
_____
_____
_____
_____

3. This is an opportune time to draw a box around this lesson's key verse in the text, "Oh, give thanks to the LORD, for He is good! For His mercy endures forever (Psalm 118:1).

Pause for Prayer

It is good for me that I have been afflicted, That I may learn Your statutes. The law of Your mouth is better to me Than thousands of coins of gold and silver (Psalm 119:71-72).

Affliction is a part of life, but you may feel you have experienced more than your share. Just as the unknown author of Psalm 118 began and ended his song by giving thanks to God, you can begin and end each day anticipating His goodness and enduring mercy through the trial you are enduring. You can begin that intimidating project at work, at home, or at church, knowing that His goodness and mercy will be with you. He sees you when you are apprehensive or in distress, when you feel unloved, and when you feel surrounded by uncertainty and hopelessness.

Lesson Eight

Perhaps you are at a good place in your life. Have you come through difficult times? You, like the psalmist, can encourage others with your testimony of deliverance.

Spend a few moments meditating on the treasures of the 15 verses you have been studying—treasures more priceless than gold and silver. Anything you have learned results from God's goodness and mercy to you. The truths you have gleaned will become more precious to you as you continue to study His Word. Bow before Him in worship, asking Him to guide your thoughts as you move into the next section.

Pulling It All Together

Psalm 118:1-14, 29 includes three elements. Identify them in the chart below.

Element	Verse Locations
Intent to Praise	
Report of Deliverance	
Concluding Praise	

Psalm 118—Praise God, His Mercy Endures Forever

Open Your Tool Box

Through diligent study, you have laid a good foundation for grasping the meaning of verses 1-14, 29 of Psalm 118. Let's consult our outside sources.

1. First, let us consult a conservative, reliable commentary, *The New International Commentary on the Old Testament* [Nancy deClaissé-Walford, Rolf A. Jacobson, Beth LaNeel Tanner, William B. Eerdmans Publishing Company], to discover how this psalm was used in Hebrew worship.

    Psalm 118 is the last of a group of psalms known as the *hallel* (or *halelûyāh*) psalms, which praise the LORD for deliverance (Psalms 111—118). More specifically, Psalms 113—118 make up "Egyptian Hallel." These six psalms were, and still are, used at the Passover meal which commemorates the Hebrews' plight in Egypt and God's deliverance from bondage. Take some time to read Psalms 113—118. Briefly summarize your conclusions below.

    _____
    _____
    _____
    _____
    _____
    _____

Lesson Eight

_____
_____
_____
_____
_____

Psalms 113 and 114 serve as community hymns to be recited before the Passover meal. Psalms 115—118 are recited at the conclusion of the meal. Two are community hymns (115, 117) and two are individual hymns of thanksgiving (116, 118). Scholars believe Psalm 118 may have been used as an entrance liturgy for the temple in Jerusalem. Envision the worshippers approaching the temple, climbing the steps, and singing this beautiful hymn of thanksgiving in unison.

2. Exodus 15 records the song Moses sang to praise God after the Israelites crossed the Red Sea and escaped from their enemies. Write Exodus 15:2 in the chart below. Then find the matching verse in Psalm 118 and write it in the second column.

Exodus 15:2	Matching Verse from Psalm 118

Psalm 118—Praise God, His Mercy Endures Forever

As you can see, God's thread of truth is woven throughout Scripture. Add this cross-reference alongside each of these verses in your Bible. This will be a valuable reminder to you as you study God's Word in the future.

3. The author opens and closes Psalm 118 with excitement and vibrant expression, thanking God because He is good and His mercy endures forever. Let us go to two excellent Bible translations and read these verses in more contemporary language:

New International Version (NIV)	New American Standard Bible (NASB)
Give thanks to the LORD, for he is good; his love endures forever.	Give thanks to the LORD, for He is good; For His lovingkindness is everlasting.

The Hebrew word that encompasses God's love is *hesed*. Notice that *mercy* is translated *love* in the NIV and *lovingkindness* in the NASB. Other expressions derived from *hesed* are "kindness, unfailing love, and great love." *The Message* paraphrases the text like this: "Thank God because he's good, because his love never quits."

4. The psalmist calls upon three groups of worshippers to celebrate the enduring lovingkindness of God. In *Psalms: Interpretation, A Bible Commentary for Teaching and Preaching*, James L. Mays declares that Psalm 118 begins with a threefold litany of invitation to Israel, priests, and God-fearers to join the individual testifier in declaring praise (or *hallel*) to the LORD.

LESSON EIGHT

5. In the Discern section, you compiled a chart of God's attributes and actions found in verses 1-14 and 29. Which of these verses introduce the congregants to the psalmist's testimony?

_____

_____

_____

6. The psalmist exclaims in verse 5 that he called on the LORD in distress. In what verses that follow does he expand on the cause of his anguish?

_____

_____

_____

7. To get an idea of how the psalmist felt in his crisis, let us do a study on the word *distress*.

- *Distress*: mêtsar, *may-tsar*; … something tight, i.e. (fig.) trouble:—distress, pain, strait. (*Strong's* 4712)

- *Mêtsar* derives from *qêbâh*.

- *Qêbâh*: *kay-baw'*; the paunch (as a cavity) or first stomach of ruminants:—maw. (*Strong's* 6896)

Merriam-Webster Dictionary defines maw as "the throat, gullet, or jaws, especially of a voracious animal." What a word picture of the psalmist's seemingly hopeless situation. He felt squeezed into a tight place, as if he were in the stomach of an animal.

Psalm 118—Praise God, His Mercy Endures Forever

8. The *distress* word study gives you another opportunity to identify a contrast in the text. Can you find the contrast in verse 5? Write it below, and record it in the text.

_____

_____

_____

9. Read verses 10–13 where the psalmist expands on his dreadful encounter. Let's compare the phrases "They surrounded me" and "I will destroy them" in several translations of the Bible.

Translation	"They surrounded me"	"I will destroy them"
King James Version	They compassed me about	Will I destroy them
New King James Version	They surround me	I will destroy them
New International Version	They surrounded me on every side They swarmed around me	I cut them down
The Message	Hemmed in by barbarians	I rubbed their faces in the dirt
The Amplified Bible	They compassed me about They surrounded me on every side They swarmed about me	I will cut them off

LESSON EIGHT

10. A word study of *destroy* will broaden your understanding of the statement, "I will destroy them."

   - *Destroy*: mûwl, *mool*; a prim. root; to cut short, i.e. curtail… by impl. to blunt; fig. to destroy. (Strong's 4135)

11. Now use some creativity to reinforce what you have learned. In your own words, rewrite verses 10-13 using terminology from your word studies.

Verse	Your Expression
10	
11	
12	
13	

12. Now return to verses 8-9. After he cried out to the LORD and the LORD answered him and set him in a broad place, what is the psalmist's conclusion?

_____
_____
_____
_____

13. A study on the words trust and confidence will shed light on the significance of these two lines.

- *Trust*: châçâh, *khaw-saw'*; ... to flee for protection [comp. 982]; fig. to confide in:—have hope, make refuge, (put) trust. (*Strong's* 2620)

- *Confidence*: bâtach, *baw-takh'*; ... to hie [go somewhere in a hurry] for refuge [but not so precipitately as 2620]; fig. to trust, be confident or sure:—be bold (confident, secure, sure)... (make to) hope, (put, make to) trust. (*Strong's* 982)

Does that clarify the psalmist's double expression of trusting God rather than man, or even princes?

My Interpretation

Your knowledge of the thanksgiving psalms continues to grow. As you further your studies, you will be glad you invested time in digging out the treasure trove of Psalm 118. Put in your own words a brief summary of how you interpret what you have learned in this lesson.

_____

_____

_____

_____

_____

_____

LESSON EIGHT

DEVOTE

Psalm 118 records a personal encounter of a man who was in a tight place. He was fearful and in distress. In his dire straits, he called on God and God answered him. God's Word is dynamic, still alive and active today. That means you can apply this thought-provoking song to your own situation to deepen your devotion and commitment to the Lord. Using the chart below, go through the text verse by verse and write a declaration of what you will do in the future when confronted by the enemy of your soul. Let God speak to you through His Word. There will be repetition, but keep going. Repetition is good!

Verse	My Resolve	My Declaration
1	I will	
5	I will	
6	I will	
7	I will	
8	I will	
9	I will	
10	I will	

Psalm 118—Praise God, His Mercy Endures Forever

11	I will	
12	I will	
13	I will	
14	I will	
29	I will	

Pause for Prayer

Your righteousness is an everlasting righteousness, And Your law is truth. Trouble and anguish have overtaken me, Yet Your commandments are my delights. The righteousness of Your testimonies is everlasting; Give me understanding, and I shall live (Psalm 119:142-144).

As you know, making a list of commitments is easy; but following through can be accomplished only by the power of the Holy Spirit. As a child of God, the Holy Spirit gives you that empowerment. Each new day offers an opportunity to determine anew that you will "Trust in the LORD with all your heart, And lean not on your own understanding; In all your ways acknowledge Him" (Proverbs 3:5, 6). If you do this, you can count on Him to "direct your paths."

Take time to pray right now. Commit to give God His rightful place in your daily walk, to give Him praise for who He is and what He has done, and to call upon Him in times of trouble.

DISCIPLE

It is exciting to hear testimonies of God's goodness and mercy in other people's lives. Such shared experiences increase your faith and give you hope when you face difficult situations.

You also have a story—a testimony. You are a witness to God's enduring love and you bear the responsibility and privilege to build up others with your witness. Read the following Scriptures and copy them out as a reminder to encourage others in their walk with the Lord.

Scripture Text	Exhortation
Hebrews 3:13	
Hebrews 10:24-25	
1 Thessalonians 5:11	
Ephesians 4:29	
Colossians 3:16	
Proverbs 27:17	

We can encourage others with our testimony in a variety of ways. Whether it's over a cup of coffee, sharing a meal, in a cell group, or a quick phone call, decide that you will build someone up in the next few days. Come up with some ideas and write them below. We've included an example on the next page to get you started.

The Person(s)	The Setting	The Message
Mary, a new woman at church	Treat Mary to coffee at a local coffee shop. Set a time limit of 60-90 minutes to respect her time and mine.	• Ask about her life and her family and how she came about attending the church. • Share some positive information about the church. • Tell her some specific ways God has used the church to minister to me. • Offer some insight about my study in the thanksgiving psalms. Invite her to attend the class. If she shows interest, call a couple of days before the next session to remind her. • Give her my phone number in case she has any questions.

LESSON EIGHT

In addition to intentionally planning to share God's goodness, be mindful of unexpected opportunities that present themselves. "Be ready in season and out of season. Exhort with all longsuffering and teaching" (2 Timothy 4:2). Remember, the Lord is your strength and your song, and He will help you.

You have completed more than half of the thanksgiving psalms studies. Your investment will be well worth it. To God be the glory!

In Lesson Nine, we will concentrate on a much shorter psalm, Psalm 138. The lessons of Psalm 118 will ring true as you uncover the riches of Psalm 138 in the next few days.

Lesson Nine

Thanksgiving

A Path to Praise

Praise God with Your Whole Heart (Psalm 138)

LESSON NINE
PSALM 138:1-8
PRAISE GOD WITH YOUR WHOLE HEART

Key Verse

I will praise You with my whole heart (Psalm 138:1).

Introduction

In Psalm 118, the psalmist began his song by calling on the congregation to join together in giving thanks to the LORD because his "mercy endures forever." In the first few stanzas, he prepared them for his testimony of Jehovah's deliverance that followed.

Psalm 118 was written for congregational worship, but the psalmist opens Psalm 138 by offering personal praise to God. At the conclusion of this lesson, you will be challenged to do likewise. With that in mind, begin with prayer, humbly asking God's blessings on your study of this uplifting psalm.

Your Exploration of the Text

Pause for Prayer

Accept, I pray, the freewill offerings of my mouth, O LORD, And teach me Your judgments... Your testimonies I have taken as a heritage forever, For they are the rejoicing of my heart (Psalm 119:108, 111).

Do you remember the term *Selah*? You learned in Lesson Three that it means to pause and reflect. As you begin Lesson Nine, pause to praise the Lord for His blessings. There is no such thing as a "mundane" blessing. Thank Him that you woke up this morning. Thank Him for every breath you take. Thank Him for every move you can make. Thank Him in advance for what you will glean from your study of Psalm 138. Do not rush this time of praise. When you are ready, move on to the joy of discovering God's Word.

THE TEXT

Psalm 138:1-8
A Psalm of David.

15:14-33

¹ I will praise You with my whole heart; Before the gods I will sing praises to You. ² I will worship toward Your holy temple, And praise Your name For Your lovingkindness and Your truth; For You have magnified Your word above all Your name. ³ In the day when I cried out, You answered me, And made me bold with strength in my soul. ⁴ All the kings of the earth shall praise You, O LORD, When they hear the words of Your mouth. ⁵ Yes, they shall sing of the ways of the LORD, For great is the glory of the LORD. ⁶ Though the LORD is on high, Yet He regards the lowly; But the proud

He knows from afar. ⁷ Though I walk in the midst of trouble, You will revive me; You will stretch out Your hand Against the wrath of my enemies, And Your right hand will save me. ⁸ The LORD will perfect that which concerns me; Your mercy, O LORD, endures forever; Do not forsake the works of Your hands.

DISCOVER

Begin reading Psalm 138 with intention. Find a quiet place without distractions and meditate on the psalmist's lyrics, receiving them as the living Word of God.

1. Silently read through the entire psalm in one sitting.

2. Purposely and prayerfully read the psalm again.

Observing the Text

As you read the psalm a third time, aloud, ask the helping questions. Record your detailed questions and answers below.

My Helping Questions and Answers

Summary. Briefly summarize your observations below.

My Findings

LESSON NINE

Every Text Has a Context

1. Record the author of the psalm below.

   _____
   _____
   _____

2. From your observations, what was David's purpose in writing this psalm?

   _____
   _____
   _____
   _____

3. One of the questions you asked as you read the text was "Who?" Identifying the characters David mentioned in this psalm will help bring his words into context. Peruse the psalm again and write below any character references, including references to the psalmist himself.

Verse	Character
1-8	
1-3, 7, 8	

Psalm 138—Praise God with Your Whole Heart

1	
4-5	
6	
6	
7	

DISCERN

Key Words Open the Door to Understanding

Read the psalm several more times, identifying repeated words and phrases and noting them in the space below. You may want to include such words as *sing*, *mercy*, *lovingkindness*, and *endures* since these key words recur throughout the Book of Psalms. Add the words and/or phrases to your list and mark them in the text with the colors and/or icons of your choice. Remember to transfer words from your previous key word lists.

_____

_____

LESSON NINE

1. As you have observed throughout your studies of the thanksgiving psalms, the LORD is always the main character. Record below the number of times He is mentioned in Psalm 138, including pronouns.

   _____

   _____

   _____

   _____

   The LORD is at the heart of David's song. Take a moment to anticipate what will be revealed to you about the Lord as you delve deeper into this text. Persevere and allow the teaching power of the Holy Spirit to speak to your heart.

2. Your main objective remains to learn all you can about the main character. As you walk through the psalm, make a list of everything you discover about the character of God.

Verse	Attributes/Actions that Reveal God's Character	Verse	Attributes/Actions that Reveal God's Character

Psalm 138—Praise God with Your Whole Heart

Take a moment to transfer these notes to the margin of your Bible.

3. References to time in Psalm 138 shed light on God's character. Mark time references in the same way you have in past lessons. Briefly explain below how the time references reveal God's character.

Verse	Time Reference	Explanation
3	<u>In the day when</u> I cried out	

4-5	<u>When</u> they (the kings of the earth) hear the words of Your mouth	
8	<u>forever</u>	

4. In verses 1 and 2, David clearly states his intentions to praise God. He answers three questions as he expresses *what* he is going to do, as well as *why* and *how* he will do it. Write his intentions below in one column and his motivation or method in the other column.

Verse	What Does He Intend to Do? (Intention)	Why or How Does He Intend to Do It? (Motivation of Method)
1		
1		
2		
2		
2		

5. After the psalmist shares his intention in verses 1-2, he elaborates on his reasons in verses 3-4. Record your observations below:

Verse	Reasons for Praising God
3	
3	
4	
5	
5	
6	
7	

Lesson Nine

7	
7	
8	
8	
8	

Notice the overlap between God's attributes, the psalmist's intentions to praise Him, and the psalmist's reasons for praising Him. Each of these reinforces the others and affirms the following:

- God is worthy to be praised.
- David has good intentions to aptly respond to the LORD.
- Because of God's character and the fact that He has proven Himself faithful, David can expect He will remain faithful in the future.

Read the psalm again to establish these affirmations in your own mind.

Psalm 138—Praise God with Your Whole Heart

Terms of Conclusion

1. In verses 2 and 5, David proclaims that the LORD will be praised, and he supports those assertions with solid reasons. Record below who will praise Him, the expression of praise, the connecting word (or term of conclusion), and why He will be praised.

Verse	Who Will Give God Praise?	Expression of Praise	Connecting Word (Term of Conclusion)	Why Will God Be Praised?
2				
5				

2. Such expressions are climactic in nature; that is, the conclusion adds excitement to what was just stated. Read verses 2 and 5 aloud, putting bold emphasis on the last line. Can you sense the depth of David's emotions as he sings this song of praise to the LORD and anticipates that the kings of the earth will join his song when they see the LORD's glory?

3. David opened this psalm with an emphatic declaration: "I will praise You with my whole heart." Draw a box around this key verse in the text.

Pause for Prayer

Revive me according to Your lovingkindness, So that I may keep the testimony of Your mouth (Psalm 119:88).

David commits to praise the LORD with his whole heart, acknowledging Him before the gods of the earth and worshipping Him toward His holy temple. Do you sense his deepening understanding of the character of the God he worships?

He cried out to God and God granted him boldness and strength in his soul. Although he anticipates that one day the kings of the earth will praise the LORD, he still expects trouble from his enemies. Because he knows his God, he can be certain of God's saving power.

That is exactly why you need to know your God. Know His character. Know His Word. When you know Him, you want to keep His Word and praise Him with your whole heart, even when difficulties loom before you or your heart is breaking.

Through your study of God's Word, you are committing to know Him. You claim the exhortation of Peter: "Grace and peace be multiplied to you in the knowledge of God and of Jesus our Lord, as His divine power has given to us all things that pertain to life and godliness, through the knowledge of Him who called us by glory and virtue, by which have been given to us exceedingly great and precious promises, that through these you may be partakers of the divine nature, having escaped the corruption that is in the world through lust… giving all diligence, add to your faith virtue, to virtue knowledge" (2 Peter 1:2-5).

Take a few moments to praise Him now. Express your passionate desire for boldness and strength to pursue Him so you can rest in your knowledge of Him when trouble shows up.

Pulling It All Together

Psalm 138 contains the elements common to the thanksgiving psalms. Identify the verse references alongside the elements listedIn the following table, list at least one core focus for this passage, other major themes you have identified, and what this passage reveals about God's nature.

Element	Verse Locations
Intent to Praise	
Report of Deliverance	
Testimony of God's Continuing Deliverance	

Lesson Nine

Open Your Tool Box

Of the six thanksgiving psalms you have studied, three were authored by David and a fourth was titled "A Song at the Dedication of the House of David." David stands as a central figure in the Book of Psalms and the Bible as a whole. You already know from David's psalms that he experienced difficult times and called out to God for help. Through a limited character study covering 15 years of his life, you will learn more about him.

Character study simply means finding out everything you can about a person. The best starting place is the Bible itself. So let us begin.

You will need your most important tool—the Bible—a pen and your colored pencils. Decide on a color and/or icon you will use to mark all references to David in your reading. An extensive character study would include finding every reference to David in the Bible by utilizing resources like an exhaustive concordance, a topical Bible, and a comprehensive cross-referencing Bible. Because of time restraints, we will choose selective Scripture readings to draw out certain highlights of David's early years. The readings are extensive, so find a comfortable spot to complete each assignment. The time you invest will be worth it. Enjoy the adventure!

1. For context, read 1 Samuel 15:10-29 to learn what led up to the events in chapter 16. Record what you discover.

Psalm 138—Praise God with Your Whole Heart

Segment	Discovery
Verses 10-16	
Verses 17-19	
Verses 20-23	
Verses 24-29	

2. Read 1 Samuel 16:1-5 and list God's instructions to Samuel and the prophet's response.

Verses	God's Instructions to Samuel and Samuel's Response
1	
2	

LESSON NINE

3	
4-5	

3. Read 1 Samuel 16:6-13 and note below the progression of Samuel's encounter with Jesse and his sons. In this chapter, mark all references to David, including pronouns. When you identified key words at the beginning of the lesson, you probably observed that David's name appeared in the title as the author of this psalm and that he spoke in first-person throughout the psalm. Continue to identify David with the same mark you used throughout Psalm 138. In verse 11, notice he is referred to as "the youngest." Be sure to mark that, as well as any other clues about who David is. On a separate sheet of paper, begin a list of everything you learn about David. Continue that list throughout this character study. You will find it invaluable for future study.

Verses	Samuel's Encounter
6-7	
8-10	

11-13	

It is worth noting that, aside from genealogies in the book of Ruth, 1 Samuel 16 contains the first mention of David in Scripture. Anything you learn here sets the stage for David's life.

4. David's relationship with Saul is a major theme throughout his early life. 1 Samuel 16:14-23 documents the beginning of that relationship. Read this selection and record the particulars of each character below.

Verses	Saul's Servants	Saul	David
14			

Lesson Nine

15-16			
17			
18			
19			

20-21			
22-23			

5. Chapter 17 documents Israel's engagement in battle with the Philistines. Verse 13 reveals that David's three eldest brothers followed Saul into battle and the next verses explain what David was doing at this time. Write verse 14 below.

_____
_____
_____
_____
_____

LESSON NINE

6. An event occurred in Chapter 17 that changed David's life forever. Read verses 17-58 and briefly summarize what happened below. Keep your observations concise, but be sure to record David's description of his qualifications.

Verses	Summary
17-22	
23-30	
31	
32-33	
34-37	
38-48	
49-57	

Psalm 138—Praise God with Your Whole Heart

7. Jonathan, Saul's son, appears in 1 Samuel 13. He plays a significant role in David's early life. Read about the start of Jonathan's friendship with David in 1 Samuel 18:1-4. List the highlights below.

Verses	Highlights of Friendship Between Jonathan and David
1	
3	
4	

8. David's miraculous victory over Goliath put him under the spotlight, and God's plan for his kingship began to unfold. Read about David's meteoric rise in 1 Samuel 18:5-7 and record your findings below.

Verses	Findings
5	

LESSON NINE

6	
7	

9. Throughout 1 Samuel, we see that David's star is rising. He skillfully played the harp to soothe King Saul. He bonded with Saul's son and made a covenant of friendship with him. He brought about victory for Israel when he killed Goliath. He thrived in a leadership position in Saul's military. The people loved David. Read 1 Samuel 18:8-12 and summarize Saul's response to David's popularity.

_____

_____

_____

_____

10. The following Scripture references reveal a number of times when Saul acted out his anger toward David. For the sake of time, we will not read the circumstances that surrounded each of Saul's actions. These excerpts will give you a clear snapshot of what David was up against from approximately 1025 B.C. until Saul's death in 1010 B.C. Read the verses listed below and note your observations.

Psalm 138—Praise God with Your Whole Heart

Text	Saul Acts Out His Anger Against David
1 Samuel 19:1, 11, 15	
1 Samuel 20:30-31	
1 Samuel 22:13-19	
1 Samuel 23:14	

11. David's response to Saul's murderous anger reveals a great deal about David's character. Read the following Scriptures and make notes.

Text	David's Response to Saul's Anger
1 Samuel 24:3-11	

LESSON NINE

1 Samuel 26:7-11	

This concludes our limited character study of David. Much of the distress referenced in his psalms resulted from Saul's mission to destroy him. In fact, Psalm 34 (Lesson Six) was inspired by a particular event when David was running from Saul. Glance back at that psalm title to refresh your memory.

If you wish to delve deeper into the life of David, a man after God's own heart (1 Samuel 13:14; Acts 13:22), the following Scriptures will get you started: 1 Samuel 16–2 Samuel; 1 Chronicles; 1 Kings 1; and the 73 psalms attributed to David.

12. Let's return to Psalm 138. In light of your character study, read the psalm again. Do you have a new perspective on David's reason for praising His creator with his whole heart?

Summary. Utilizing what you have learned about this psalm and its author, describe what you think Psalm 138 meant to David when he wrote it.

My Interpretation

_____
_____
_____
_____
_____
_____
_____
_____
_____
_____

DEVOTE

Your character study of David revealed that he desired to please God. He was dismayed that Goliath would "defy the armies of the living God" (1 Samuel 17:26). He glorified God when he declared "The battle is the LORD's" (v. 47). Although Saul acted out his jealousy by trying to take David's life, David took the high road and refused to kill Saul when he had the opportunity. He spared "the LORD's anointed" (1 Samuel 26:9) and declared "As the LORD lives, the LORD shall strike him, or his day shall come to die, or he shall go out to battle and perish. The LORD forbid that I should stretch out my hand against the LORD's anointed" (vv. 10, 11).

You must decide how you will behave when distraught over world conditions, personal conflict, attacks by Satan, and the like. Determine now that you will take the high road and defend truth and righteousness, according to God's Word. Make up your mind that you will have confidence, knowing that the battle is the Lord's. Commit right now to praise the Lord with your whole heart in the midst of the "gods" of this world.

Pause for Prayer

Let Your mercies come also to me, O LORD—Your salvation according to Your word. So shall I have an answer for him who reproaches me, For I trust in Your word... I will speak of Your testimonies also before kings, And will not be ashamed (Psalm 119:41, 42, 46).

Turn your face toward heaven, and praise God with your whole heart. Do not rush through this time with the Lord. In fact, return to Psalm 138 and pray through this amazing thanksgiving psalm. Focus on God's character and claim the last verse for yourself. Trust Him to perfect that which concerns you and perform His work in you to bring it to completion for His glory. Cling to the knowledge that you are the work of His hands and He will not forsake you.

DISCIPLE

Just as God had a work for David to do, He has a work for you to do.

In his contemplative Psalm 78:70-72, Asaph expresses God's choice of David to lead the nation of Israel:

He also chose David His servant, And took him from the sheepfolds; From following the ewes that had young He brought him, To shepherd Jacob His people, And Israel His inheritance. So he shepherded them according to the integrity of his heart, And guided them by the skillfulness of his hands.

From your character study of David, recall that Samuel visited the house of Jesse in Bethlehem to anoint one of his sons to replace Saul as king. God revealed to Samuel that He had not chosen any of those who were in the house, so he asked whether there were any other sons. It was only then that Jesse mentioned his youngest son in the field tending sheep. God knew where David was all the time because He had "sought for Himself a man after His own heart" (1 Samuel 13:14). He knew the integrity of David's heart and the skillfulness of his hands. In short, he knew David's potential—who he *could* be.

How fitting that David composed Psalm 139, declaring, "Where can I go from Your Spirit? Or where can I flee from Your presence?" (v. 7). Read Psalm 139:1-18 and accept its truths for yourself.

LESSON NINE

You are not too young or too old to embrace the work God wants to complete in you. Your station in life is not too low or too high—God wants to use you where you are. Remember the words of the Lord to Samuel, "Do not look at his appearance or at his physical stature… For the LORD does not see as man sees, for man looks at the outward appearance, but the LORD looks at the heart" (1 Samuel 16:7). You are the work of His hands, fearfully and wonderfully made. Praise Him because you are one of a kind, skillfully formed by Him, and He sees your heart.

Take some time now to humbly assess your background, your disposition, your experiences, your strengths, your weaknesses, and your roles in various areas of your life (work, home, church, community). Commit all those things to Him and decide that you are going to prayerfully strive to reach your God-given potential for His glory. Maybe God wants to use you as a prayer warrior for someone else. Perhaps there is a leadership role He intends for you to fill. He may choose you to teach children or conduct a neighborhood Bible study. God chose a shepherd boy to become a king. What does He want you to become?

Being part of God's plan gives you freedom and joy that will overflow in worship, either alone or among a community of believers. Keep in mind that David did not attain kingship for 15 years after his anointing. God's timing is always perfect. Keep pursuing Him through His Word and prayer, and trust Him for what He has in store for you.

In Lesson Ten, you will join with a host of worshippers giving thanks to the Lord for His goodness and His wonderful works to the children of men.

Lesson Ten

Thanksgiving

A Path to Praise

Praise God, He Delivers From Distress (Psalm 107)

LESSON TEN

PSALM 107:1-32

PRAISE GOD, HE DELIVERS FROM DISTRESS

Key Verse

Then they cried out to the Lord in their trouble, And He delivered them out of their distresses (Psalm 107:6).

Introduction

Lesson Nine focused on a personal worship experience. The account of David's ascent to Israel's throne has been preserved for us in the Holy Scriptures. In your attentive study of Psalm 138, you used David's inspired words in your time of devotion and committed to live out what you learned.

In this lesson, we will transition from individual thanksgiving to community thanksgiving. The nation of Israel often gathered together for corporate worship. As an agricultural society, they gathered to give thanks for God's blessings during harvest. As a nation assaulted by many enemies, they gathered give thanks for God's deliverance. As the chosen nation of the loving God, they gathered to give thanks for God's providential care. The community-oriented thanksgiving psalms helped them express gratitude during congregational worship.

Psalm 107 is replete with examples of God's redemptive acts toward His people. The psalmist skillfully and powerfully calls the community to join together and thank the living God with one voice.

Time and space restraints require us to limit our study of Psalm 107 to the first 32 verses.

Your Exploration of the Text

Pause for Prayer

I will praise You with uprightness of heart, When I learn Your righteous judgments. I will keep Your statutes; Oh, do not forsake me utterly! (Psalm 119:7, 8).

Do you recall the opening and closing words of the psalmist in Psalm 118? "Oh, give thanks to the LORD, for He is good! For His mercy endures forever." This praise rings out again in Psalm 107 as the psalmist opens a time of community thanksgiving. This recurrent theme in Scripture emphasizes two aspects of God's character: goodness and mercy. Has your study in the thanksgiving psalms made you more aware of the goodness and mercy of the Lord in your life?

PSALM 107—PRAISE GOD, HE DELIVERS FROM DISTRESS

This prayer of thanksgiving in Psalm 107:1 would be an excellent way to begin your prayer time today as you prepare to embrace the message God has in store for you. His throne room is open and He is ready to receive your praises. Enter into His presence by the power of the Holy Spirit and, after a time of thanksgiving, ask Him to lead you into all truth as you increase in knowledge through His Word.

THE TEXT

Psalm 107:1-32

¹ Oh, give thanks to the LORD, for He is good! For His mercy endures forever. ² Let the redeemed of the LORD say so, Whom He has redeemed from the hand of the enemy, ³ And gathered out of the lands, From the east and from the west, From the north and from the south. ⁴ They wandered in the wilderness in a desolate way; They found no city to dwell in. ⁵ Hungry and thirsty, Their soul

fainted in them. ⁶ Then they cried out to the LORD in their trouble, And He delivered them out of their distresses. ⁷ And He led them forth by the right way, That they might go to a city for a dwelling place. ⁸ Oh, that men would give thanks to the LORD for His goodness, And for His wonderful works to the children of men! ⁹ For He satisfies the longing soul, And fills the hungry soul with goodness.

¹⁰ Those who sat in darkness and in the shadow of death, Bound in affliction and irons— ¹¹ Because they rebelled against the words of God, And despised the counsel of the Most High, ¹² Therefore He brought down their heart with labor; They fell down, and there was none to help. ¹³ Then they cried out to the LORD in their trouble, And He saved them out of their distresses. ¹⁴ He brought them out of darkness and the shadow of death, And broke their chains in pieces. ¹⁵ Oh, that men would give thanks to the LORD for His goodness, And for His wonderful works to the children of men! ¹⁶ For He has

broken the gates of bronze, And cut the bars of iron in two. ¹⁷ Fools, because of their transgression, And because of their iniquities, were afflicted. ¹⁸ Their soul abhorred all manner of food, And they drew near to the gates of death. ¹⁹ Then they cried out to the LORD in their trouble, And He saved them out of their distresses. ²⁰ He sent His word and healed them, And delivered them from their destructions.²¹ Oh, that men would give thanks to the LORD for His goodness, And for His wonderful works to the children of men! ²² Let them sacrifice the sacrifices of thanksgiving, And declare His works with rejoicing. ²³ Those who go down to the sea in ships, Who do business on great waters, ²⁴ They see the works of the LORD, And His wonders in the deep. ²⁵ For He commands and raises the stormy wind, Which lifts up the waves of the sea. ²⁶ They mount up to the heavens, They go down again to the depths; Their soul melts because of trouble. ²⁷ They reel to and fro, and stagger like a drunken man, And are at their wits' end. ²⁸ Then they cry out to the LORD in their trouble, And He brings them out of their distresses. ²⁹ He calms the storm, So that its waves are still. ³⁰ Then they are glad because they are quiet; So He guides them to their desired haven. ³¹ Oh, that men would give thanks to the LORD for His goodness, And for His wonderful works to the children of men! ³² Let them exalt Him also in the assembly of the people, And praise Him in the company of the elders.

DISCOVER

1. Read Psalm 107:1-32 in one sitting.

2. As you read the text a second time, observe the rhythm of this psalm that was intended to be sung by a community of worshippers. Notice how the cadence intensifies with repeated exclamations of praise.

3. Read the psalm aloud this time, noting the statements the psalmist repeats to draw the congregation into worship. Add your own inflections to achieve the psalmist's desired effect.

Psalm 107—Praise God, He Delivers from Distress

Pay special attention to the helping questions. Record your specific helping questions and answers below.

My Helping Questions and Answers

Lesson Ten

Summary. Briefly summarize your observations below.

My Findings

_____
_____
_____
_____
_____
_____
_____
_____
_____
_____
_____

Every Text Has a Context

1. Two of the first observations you make when studying the thanksgiving psalms are the psalm's title and author. What did you notice about those two things in this psalm?

   _____
   _____

PSALM 107—PRAISE GOD, HE DELIVERS FROM DISTRESS 271

2. At the outset of this lesson, you learned that Psalm 107 is a community psalm. Now that you have read it several times, what evidence of this have you found?

_____
_____
_____
_____
_____
_____

3. List the first mention of every character or group the psalmist references in Psalm 107.

Verses	Character
1	
2	
8	
8	
9	
17	
23	

LESSON TEN

DISCERN

Key words Open the Door to Understanding

Repeated words, phrases, and sentences offer a great deal of insight into the heart of this psalm. Add these to your key word list and mark them in the text with the colors and/or icons of your choice. Remember to transfer words from your previous key word lists.

_____
_____
_____
_____
_____
_____

1. Count the number of times the LORD and pronouns referring to Him appear in the text and make note of the number below.

_____
_____
_____
_____
_____
_____

Psalm 107—Praise God, He Delivers from Distress

2. The One who inspired this community thanksgiving psalm is clear. Glean all you can about Him in this passage and list those discoveries on the chart below.

Verse	Attributes/Actions that Reveal God's Character	Verse	Attributes/Actions that Reveal God's Character

LESSON TEN

If time permits, transfer these attributes and actions to the margin of your Bible.

3. Peruse the text for references to time and mark them as you did in past lessons. One word you may not immediately view as a time reference is *then*. Notice that each expression of *then* follows a certain incident. Something happened and after that—or *then*—something else happened. This helps you answer the question of "When?" in the text. On the chart below, briefly record each incident and what happened afterward.

Verse	The Situation	Time Reference	What Followed
4-7		then	
10, 12-14		then	
17-18		then	
25-30		then	

4. Perhaps you realized through this exercise that the psalmist divided his song into four categories of crisis and deliverance, ending each section with a call to praise. He reflects on various tragedies that came upon those who experienced the Babylonian destruction of Jerusalem and Judah (598-586 B.C.). Many of the Hebrews were taken into exile and many others fled in all directions to

Psalm 107—Praise God, He Delivers from Distress

escape the devastation. Psalm 107's four vignettes of tragedy and deliverance collectively depict God's gracious deliverance of the people of Israel from the afflictions of Babylonian oppression. Each vignette follows a similar literary pattern illustrating the lovingkindness of Jehovah God.

Beginning in verse 4, thoughtfully read each vignette and identify the group, their crisis, their response to the crisis, and the LORD's response to them. This will reinforce the work you have already done and put it in perspective. We've included an example to get you started.

Notice that there is a connecting word, or term of conclusion, following the call to praise at the end of the first two sections. Record the reason for praising the LORD and underline the connecting word. The last two sections give a response to the call to praise. Write that verse in the space provided.

GROUP 1: **Verses: 4-9**	They wandered in the wilderness in a desolate way; They found no city to dwell in. Hungry and thirsty, Their soul fainted in them (vv. 4, 5).		
Verses	**Crisis**	**Response to Crisis**	**LORD's Response**
4-7	Wamdered in wilderness, desolate; no city to dwell in; hungry, thirsty; soul fainted in them	Cried out to the LORD in their trouble	He delivered them out of their distresses. He led them forth by the right way, That they might go to a city for a dwelling place.

Lesson Ten

CALL TO PRAISE: Verse: 8	Oh, that men would give thanks to the LORD for His goodness, And for His wonderful works to the children of men!
REASON FOR PRAISING THE LORD: Verse: 9	<u>For</u> He satisfies the longing soul, And fills the hungry soul with goodness.

GROUP 2: **Verses: 10-16**			
Verses	Crisis	Response to Crisis	LORD's Response

CALL TO PRAISE:
Verse: 8

REASON FOR PRAISING THE LORD:
Verse:

Psalm 107—Praise God, He Delivers from Distress

GROUP 3: Verses: 17-22			
Verses	**Crisis**	**Response to Crisis**	**LORD's Response**

CALL TO PRAISE:
Verse: 8

REASON FOR PRAISING THE LORD:
Verse:

Lesson Ten

GROUP 4: Verses: 25-32			
Verses	**Crisis**	**Response to Crisis**	**LORD's Response**

CALL TO PRAISE:
Verse: 8

REASON FOR PRAISING THE LORD:
Verse:

5. In your Scripture text, draw a box around the key verse. This verse recurs throughout the psalm with slightly different verbiage (vv. 6, 13, 19, 28). Draw a box in the same color around each of those verses. Indicate in the margin that verse 6 is the key verse.

Pause for Prayer

I thought about my ways, And turned my feet to Your testimonies. I made haste, and did not delay To keep Your commandments. The cords of the wicked have bound me, But I have not forgotten Your law (Psalm 119:59-61).

In each of the four vignettes illustrated in this psalm, the people found themselves in distress. Each time, they cried out to the LORD and each time, He provided what they needed and delivered them. The repeated cry of the psalmist expresses a longing: "Oh, that men would give thanks to the LORD for His goodness, And for His wonderful works to the children of men!"

Can you think of times in your life when God Most High delivered you from trouble? Do you praise Him often for His goodness and wonderful works to you? Do so now and tell Him of your desire for a growing relationship with Him.

As you pray, review the chart on which you listed God's attributes and actions revealing His character. Take your time and give Him praise. When you are ready, move on to the next section.

Pulling It All Together

The author sprinkled Psalm 107 with reports of deliverance following cries for help. Verses 32-43 include a testimony of God's continuing deliverance, but we are not covering those verses in this lesson. Take time to read those verses in your Bible. Then complete the chart below.

Element	Verse Locations
Intent to Praise	
Reports of Deliverance	
Concluding Praise	vv.32-43

Open Your Tool Box

Have you participated in a church service during which responsive readings were used or men and women sang alternating verses of a song? Psalm 107 is liturgical in nature, using similar techniques to draw the congregation into worship. The worship leader used a ritual, or specific method, to engage the people in praising the Lord.

While we cannot absolutely ascertain the inspiration for the psalmist's word pictures, we know that the people were redeemed from the hand of the enemy. They had been lost, bound in darkness, afflicted and near death, and in the midst of severe storms. In each case, their situation seemed hopeless and their recourse was to cry out to the Lord. The Lord delivered them every time and their freedom evoked praise.

PSALM 107—PRAISE GOD, HE DELIVERS FROM DISTRESS

My Interpretation

You most likely feel you have just scratched the surface of Psalm 107 and is the beauty of inductive Bible study. You tiptoe into the waters and continue to wade in a little at a time. "Oh, the depth of the riches both of the wisdom and knowledge of God! How unsearchable are His judgments and His ways past finding out!" (Romans 11:33).

Consider what you have gleaned from the riches of this psalm. Record your interpretation below from the perspective of the psalmist and the worshippers.

_____
_____
_____
_____
_____
_____
_____
_____
_____
_____
_____
_____

DEVOTE

Psalm 107 has been called "The Lyric of Lovingkindness." What an apt description of this song devoted to God's redemption and deliverance of His people from distress! The psalmist said it well in Psalm 118:5: "I called on the LORD in distress; The LORD answered me and set me in a broad place."

From what has the Lord delivered you? From what do you still need to be rescued? You may not have been wandering in a desert, but have you found yourself in spiritual dry places, thirsty and hungry for a deeper relationship with the Lord? Perhaps you have never been chained in a dark prison, but have you been bound by fear, depression, negativism, a critical spirit, pornography, drugs, or anything else? Are you sick with worry? Do you struggle with guilt from poor choices, failures, or past sins? Are you overcome by the storms of life, reeling to and fro, at your wits' end?

Let God's Word speak to you through the power of the Holy Spirit. Then speak to your heavenly Father. You have an Advocate, the Lord Jesus Christ, who intercedes for you.

Pause for Prayer

And I will walk at liberty, For I seek Your precepts (Psalm 119:45).

Maybe you love the Lord, but you've been searching for peace in the wrong places. Do you have a void in your life? Continue to study His Word and seek Him in prayer, asking Him to fill that void.

"As the deer pants for the water brooks, So pants my soul for You, O God. My soul thirsts for God, for the living God" (Psalm 42:1, 2).

DISCIPLE

Do you think all of the worshippers singing Psalm 107 were paying attention? Perhaps they merely recited the lyrics by rote, a host of other things closing in on their thoughts. "Oh, that men would give thanks to the LORD for His goodness, And for His wonderful works to the children of men!" Did some of the participants fail to grasp the psalmist's earnest plea in this refrain?

God deserves your praise. His goodness and mercy beckon you to worship Him from your heart. At times, your busyness may distract you from His keeping power in your everyday life.

Using the vignettes in Psalm 107, think about the ways God keeps providing for you in the good and bad times. Keep a journal of your thoughts for the next few days and the next time you join in congregational worship, respond wholeheartedly to the psalmist's appeal to give thanks to the Lord. Let the redeemed of the Lord say so! Engage in worship for your own benefit and as an example to those around you but, most of all, do it for the Lord!

We will study another community thanksgiving psalm in Lesson Eleven, joining the Israelites to praise God, our help in times of need.

284 LESSON TEN

Lesson Eleven

Thanksgiving

A Path to Praise

Praise God, Our Help In Times of Need (Psalm 124)

LESSON ELEVEN

PSALM 124:1-8

PRAISE GOD, OUR HELP IN TIMES OF NEED

Key Verse

Our help is in the name of the LORD, Who made heaven and earth (Psalm 124:8).

Introduction

The Lord is on our side! What an uplifting way to begin our final study from the Book of Psalms. You uncovered some awesome truths about God's deliverance in our last lesson. Four times the psalmist declared that the people cried out to the LORD and He delivered them out of distress. Four times he called for them to give thanks to the LORD for His goodness and His wonderful works to the children of men.

You spent time meditating on ways God has delivered you and seeking Him to free you from bondage. You responded by praising Him and journaling your thoughts of Him.

Now let's turn to another community thanksgiving psalm. The Israelites had so much for which to praise the Lord. The psalmists used their God-given, Holy Spirit-inspired creativity to open the eyes of the Israelites and broaden their understanding of the Lord's blessings.

Pause for Prayer

I cry out to You; Save me, and I will keep Your testimonies. I rise before the dawning of the morning, And cry for help; I hope in Your word (Psalm 119:146, 147).

Trouble comes. The Israelites experienced it over and over again and God came to their rescue when they cried out for help. This thanksgiving psalm reminds the reader of God's intervention in the midst of hopelessness.

PSALM 124 —PRAISE GOD, OUR HELP IN TIMES OF NEED

THE TEXT

Psalm 124:1-8
A Song of Ascents. Of David.

¹ "If it had not been the LORD who was on our side," Let Israel now say— ² "If it had not been the LORD who was on our side, When men rose up against us, ³ Then they would have swallowed us alive, When their wrath was kindled against us; ⁴ Then the waters would have overwhelmed us, The stream would have gone over our soul; ⁵ Then the swollen waters Would have gone over our soul."

⁶ Blessed be the LORD, Who has not given us as prey to their teeth. ⁷ Our soul has escaped as a bird from the snare of the fowlers; The snare is broken, and we have escaped. ⁸ Our help is in the name of the LORD, Who made heaven and earth.

LESSON ELEVEN

DISCOVER

In a sense, you have been mining the thanksgiving psalms—excavating them and digging out treasures one by one. While Psalm 124 is not lengthy, it overflows with riches you can apply to your own life.

1. Meditate as you read through Psalm 124 for the first time. Quietly think about each line, inspired by the Holy Spirit and preserved for your benefit.

2. Read the text again, paying attention to the title and the "what if" the psalmist presents to the nation of Israel.

3. Read the psalm aloud this time, passionately enunciating the words *if* and *then*. Pay special attention to the helpings questions. As you read, record your specific helping questions and answers below.

My Helping Questions and Answers

_____
_____
_____
_____
_____
_____

Summary. Briefly summarize your observations below.

My Findings

Lesson Eleven

Every Text Has a Context

1. Note any details you learn from the title of Psalm 124.

   _____
   _____
   _____
   _____

2. Just like Psalm 107, Psalm 124 is a community psalm. What details in the text confirm this?

   _____
   _____
   _____
   _____

3. List any characters mentioned in this psalm.

Verse	Character
1, 2, 6, 8	
1	
2, 7	

PSALM 124 —PRAISE GOD, OUR HELP IN TIMES OF NEED

DISCERN

Key Words Open the Door to Understanding

Recognizing key words in the text is probably becoming easier for you, both inside and outside of this inductive study. Key words emphasize the message being conveyed. Carefully walk through Psalm 124 and mark key words and phrases. Record them below and add them to your key word list, marking them in the text with the colors and/or icons of your choice. Transfer similar words from your previous key word lists.

_____

_____

_____

_____

1. Once again, the LORD stands at the center of this psalm, although His name appears far fewer times than in previous psalms you have studied. How many times is *the LORD*, including pronouns, mentioned? Compare that to the number of verses in this psalm.

_____

_____

_____

_____

Lesson Eleven

2. What does this psalm reveal about the LORD?

Verse	Revelation of God's Character
1-2	
2-3	
4-5	
6	
6-7	
7	
8	
8	

3. Transfer these attributes and actions to the margin of your Bible.

4. Like Psalm 107, Psalm 124 is liturgical in nature. What characteristics qualify this psalm as liturgical?

_____
_____
_____
_____
_____
_____

5. Time references tell a story in Psalm 124. Complete the chart below with any time references you find. We've included an example to get you started.

Verse	Introductory Clause	Time Reference	Concern/Fear
2	If it had not been the LORD who was on our side	when	men rose up against us
3		then	they would have swallowed us alive
3		when	their wrath was kindled against us
4			
5			

6. The psalmist described Israel's plight using graphic metaphors. Then he concluded the psalm using the same literary technique. Complete the chart below.

Verse	Introductory Clause	Reason for Praise
6	Blessed be the Lord	Who has not given us as prey to their teeth
7		
7		
8		

7. A *simile* is a figure of speech that draws a comparison between two different things, often using connecting words such as *like*, *as*, or *such as*. Similes create mental pictures that bring the text to life. Can you identify the simile in verse 7?

First Clause	Connecting Word	Second Clause

8. The psalmist repeats a key phrase that is critical to Israel's understanding of why they were able to escape the peril brought upon them. Write that phrase in space provided:

Psalm 124 — Praise God, Our Help in Times of Need

_____
_____
_____
_____
_____
_____
_____

Pause for Prayer

They draw near who follow after wickedness; They are far from Your law. You are near, O LORD, And all Your commandments are truth. Concerning Your testimonies, I have known of old that You have founded them forever (Psalm 119:150-152).

Once again, you have been immersed in a message of hope from the Word of God. You witnessed hope lived out in your character study of David, and you can see hope in this community psalm. While hope may not appear to be an obvious theme, we can infer that the Lord's deliverance from trouble gives the Israelites hope for the future. Their hope rings out in verse 8 when they declare, "Our help is in the name of the LORD, Who made heaven and earth."

Before you move on, be still before the Lord. Perhaps you feel overwhelmed. Maybe you can relate to the distress David described. Ask the Lord to give you understanding and assurance that your Creator God is in control.

Lesson Eleven

Pulling It All Together

Psalm 124 includes the elements common to thanksgiving psalms. Locate the references and record them below.

Element	Verse Locations
Intent to Praise	
Report of Deliverance	
Concluding Praise	

My Interpretation

Consider how much you can glean from Scripture by looking at Scripture alone. Isn't it wonderful to know that God can speak to you personally through His Word? It is important, however, to think about David's psalm in its original context. Picture yourself in the midst of the Israelites ascending to the temple, joining the worship leader in song. Try to wrap your mind around how much the worship experience was influenced by the Israelites' history and lifestyle. Then write your interpretation in your own words.

_____

_____

_____

Open Your Tool Box

Now let us consider what Bible scholars say about this Song of Ascents penned by David.

Psalms 120—134 are categorized as Songs of Ascents. James L. Mays asserts that the title most likely refers to the journeys made by pilgrims to the three annual festivals observed in Jerusalem, as described in Deuteronomy 16:16. The verb *ascend* speaks of the journey to Jerusalem. Because Jerusalem is about 2500 feet above sea level, the pilgrims ascended, or went up, to Jerusalem from any given geographical location. Once the pilgrims reached Jerusalem, they would make the trek up to the temple. The Songs of Ascent were most likely used in the journey or in processionals during the festivals.

Lesson Eleven

For more insight into the ascent to Jerusalem, read the following excerpts from the Songs of Ascents and note anything you learn about Jerusalem.

Scripture	Your Thoughts
Psalm 121:1-2 I will lift up my eyes to the hills— From whence comes my help? My help comes from the LORD, Who made heaven and earth.	
Psalm 125:1-2 Those who trust in the LORD Are like Mount Zion, Which cannot be moved, but abides forever. As the mountains surround Jerusalem, So the LORD surrounds His people From this time forth and forever.	
Psalm 128:5-6 The LORD bless you out of Zion, And may you see the good of Jerusalem All the days of your life. Yes, may you see your children's children.	

Psalm 124 — Praise God, Our Help in Times of Need

Notice the references to Zion. Bible scholars agree that Zion and Jerusalem are synonymous throughout the Bible.

The psalmist's use of language teems with symbolism that would have spoken vividly to the pilgrims making their way to Jerusalem. You probably marked a phrase that was repeated twice at the beginning of the psalm: "If it had not been the LORD who was on our side." For obvious reasons, this is called an "if clause" and contains a condition. As you can see, it introduces a series of phrases that explain the consequences of the condition. Record below what would have happened "if it had not been the LORD who was on our side."

The Condition	Verses	The Consequences
If it had not been the LORD who was on our side	2-3	
	3-5	

As Mays explains, "Waters that engulf or sweep away are a frequent image for personal and corporate danger; the image evokes the sense of a power before which one is helpless."

Further imagery in verses 6 and 7 evokes the dire straits in which the Israelites found themselves and their subsequent rescue. Break down the striking description in the space provided.

LESSON ELEVEN

Verse	Praise to the LORD	Description
6b	Blessed be the LORD,	
7a		
7b		

A bird caught in a snare was another familiar image for the time and place in which Psalm 124 was written. Once again, the psalmist effectively describes the distress of the people of Israel and God's redeeming work in their lives. Mays asserts that the psalmist's word pictures were not "composed to tell what happened but to dramatize how great was the great danger and narrow the escape."

Re-read Psalm 124:8. As you learned early in your studies of the thanksgiving psalms, *LORD* is the Hebrew *Yehôvâh*. The second part of verse 8 describes another of the LORD's qualities; Creator, or *Elohim*. Although the name *Elohim* is not listed each time one of God's creative acts is revealed in the Holy Scriptures, each use of the word reveals the creative nature of His character. It is important for a student of the Word to have an understanding of His name as Elohim. This name first appears in Genesis 1:1. Write the verse in the space provided.

Psalm 124 — Praise God, Our Help in Times of Need

_____
_____
_____
_____

Let's refer to *The New Strong's Exhaustive Concordance of the Bible* for the definition of *Elohim*, as used in Genesis 1:1.

- God: ʼĕlôhîym, *el-o-heem'*; …gods in ordinary sense; but spec. used (in the plur...) of the supreme God. (*Strong's* 430)

Did you notice that Genesis 1:1 uses the supreme God's name in the *plural*? This affirms the plurality of the Godhead as it appears in Genesis 1:26. Record that verse below.

_____
_____
_____

We have reason to rejoice in the truth of the blessed Trinity—God the Father, God the Son, and God the Holy Spirit. Record Deuteronomy 6:4 and 10:17 below.

Deut. 6:4
Deut. 10:17

Where you see *God* in these verses, He is called *Elohim*, the Creator of heaven and earth. Where *LORD* is used, He is called *Jehovah*, the self-existent, eternal One.

Return to Psalm 124:8. When you listed the attributes of God's character in the Discern section, did you name Him as Creator? If not, go back and do so now.

DEVOTE

The theme of hope recurs throughout the Book of Psalms. *The New Strong's Exhaustive Concordance of the Bible* illuminates the meaning of *hope* as understood by the psalmists with the Hebrew words *yâchal* and *tôw cheleth*: "to wait; by implication, to be patient; be pained, tarry, trust; expectation." Expectation, yes! But patience? Pain? It is not easy to endure those. After all, no one wants to feel they are "being swallowed alive" or are in "the snare of the fowlers." David, the shepherd boy anointed to be king, had been there. He could share not only the distress but also the hope: "If it had not been the LORD who was on our side… Our help is in the name of the LORD, Who made heaven and earth." How could he share that hope? He had a testimony of deliverance.

Devote some time to reflecting on your testimony of deliverance. Think about how you felt when you were going through a time of waiting or pain. Recall how you trusted God for the outcome. Remember how He brought you through.

Are you in the middle of a crisis now? Saturate yourself in God's Word. Call out to Him in prayer. Heighten your expectations and wait on Him.

Pause for Prayer

Remember the word to Your servant, Upon which You have caused me to hope. This is my comfort in my affliction, For Your word has given me life... Your statutes have been my songs In the house of my pilgrimage. I remember Your name in the night, O LORD, And I keep Your law. This has become mine, Because I kept Your precepts (Psalm 119:49, 50, 54, 55).

Remember. David was remembering when he penned Psalm 124. He recalled fierce attacks on the nation of Israel and this was a song of hope for them. It is also a song of hope for you and other Christ followers every day. "Be sober, be vigilant; because your adversary the devil walks about like a roaring lion, seeking whom he may devour. Resist him, steadfast in the faith, knowing that the same sufferings are experienced by your brotherhood in the world" (1 Peter 5:8, 9).

Meditate on Psalm 119:49, 50, 54, 55 and 1 Peter 5:8, 9. Pray for an open heart and an open mind as you make a commitment at the end of this lesson.

DISCIPLE

Suffering comes in many forms—persecution, addictions, fear, illness, family discord, and a host of other maladies. We bring some hardship on ourselves through poor choices or disobedience. Others are consequences of a fallen world. As a result, we each have many needs. As a believer, you carry hope in a fallen world.

God remembers His perpetual promises recorded in His living Word. Through prayer and action, through the power of the Holy Spirit, you can bring those promises to life. Ask God for wisdom and guidance. How can He can use you to help meet some of those needs in a practical way?

Commit to pray for your needs and the needs of others. You could make a weekly prayer list, titling columns with prayer topics, such as personal, family, friends, church leaders, missions, community, and government. Then determine to pray for a different category each day of the week. Do not be legalistic. Make changes as necessary.

Always begin and end your prayer time with praise to God, our help in times of need! Praise anticipates and celebrates God's lovingkindness.

Look forward with anticipation to Lesson Twelve. You will study the experience of a man in great distress. Do you remember what you learned in Lesson Eight (Psalm 118) about the meaning of distress from the Hebrew words mêtsar and qêbâh? Distress refers to something "tight, i.e. (fig.)

trouble: distress, pain, strait; the paunch (as a cavity) or first stomach of ruminants." Lesson Twelve focuses on the psalm Jonah prayed to the Lord literally from a fish's belly.

Grab your excavating gear and prepare to mine the treasures in Jonah 2, your last thanksgiving psalm.

Lesson Twelve

Thanksgiving

A Path to Praise

Praise God, He delivers from death (Jonah 2)

LESSON TWELVE

JONAH 2:1-10

Key Verse

But I will sacrifice to You With the voice of thanksgiving; I will pay what I have vowed. Salvation is of the Lord (Jonah 2:9).

Introduction

As we come to the conclusion of our study in the thanksgiving psalms, it seems appropriate to conclude with a study of one such psalm in its historical context. The individual psalms in the Book of Psalms rarely give us enough detail to identify their historical setting with certainty. The closest we come to knowing about the historical event that sparked the psalm is any brief information found in some of the psalm titles (e.g., Psalm 51). However, numerous places in Scripture record expressions of thanksgiving. When Israel came out of Egypt at the Exodus, the people of Israel sang a song of thanksgiving to God (Exodus 15:1-18). David expressed his thanks to God for the many times he was spared from his enemies (2 Samuel 22). King Hezekiah gave thanks to God for divine healing that extended his life for many more years (Isaiah 38:9-20).

One of the most unusual songs of thanksgiving comes from the prophet Jonah. His expression of gratitude has many similarities to the thanksgiving psalms. The study in this lesson will enable you to see more clearly the relationship between God's saving acts and the psalms that celebrate and testify to such divine care.

Your Exploration of the Text

Pause for Prayer

> *My soul clings to the dust; Revive me according to Your word. I have declared my ways, and You answered me; Teach me Your statutes… My soul melts from heaviness; Strengthen me according to Your word* (Psalm 119:25, 26, 28).

As you approach God in prayer, preparing to interpret His Word, be reminded that Jonah's problem was self-inflicted. Jonah ended up in a situation that directly resulted from his disobedience to God. But even in such a situation, God chose to forgive Jonah's sin and deliver him. Read Jonah 1 before you pray. God's response to Jonah reminds us of John's exhortation to us: "If we confess our sins, [God] is faithful and just to forgive us our sins and to cleanse us from all unrighteousness" (1 John 1:9). As you pray, may God increase your awareness of His grace in your own life and in the lives of others around you. Ask the Holy Spirit to enable you to discern how the message of Jonah 2 can speak to you.

THE TEXT

Jonah 2:1-10

¹ Then Jonah prayed to the LORD his God from the fish's belly. ² And he said: "I cried out to the LORD because of my affliction, And He answered me. "Out of the belly of Sheol I cried, And You heard my voice. ³ For You cast me into the deep. Into the heart of the seas, And the floods surrounded me; All Your billows and Your waves passed over me. ⁴ Then I said, 'I have been cast out of Your sight; Yet I will look again toward Your holy temple.' ⁵ The waters surrounded me, even to my soul; The deep closed around me; Weeds were wrapped around my head. ⁶ I went down to the moorings of the mountains; The earth with its bars closed behind me forever; Yet You have brought up my life from the pit, O LORD, my God. ⁷ "When my soul fainted within me, I remembered the LORD; And

my prayer went up to You, Into Your holy temple. ⁸ "Those who regard worthless idols Forsake their own Mercy. ⁹ But I will sacrifice to You With the voice of thanksgiving; I will pay what I have vowed. Salvation is of the LORD." ¹⁰ So the LORD spoke to the fish, and it vomited Jonah onto dry land.

DISCOVER

The thanksgiving psalm in Jonah 2 forms an important connecting link between Jonah 1 and Jonah 3—4. Chapter 1 provides critical answers to our helping questions.

Silently read through Jonah 2 in its entirety. Prayerfully read the chapter again. You will discover the historical context for Jonah's song as you work through the exercises below.

My Helping Questions and Answers

1. Read Jonah 1 and answer the following questions.

   a. Who was Jonah?

   _____
   _____
   _____

Jonah 2 — Praise God, He Delivers from Death

b. What task did God commission Jonah to do?

c. Where did Jonah live?

d. Where did God tell Jonah to go and preach?

e. Where did Jonah try to go?

f. When did Jonah minister?

LESSON TWELVE

   g. Why did God commission Jonah to go and preach?

   _____

   _____

   _____

   _____

   h. Why did Jonah disobey God?

   _____

   _____

   _____

   _____

   i. How is Jonah 2 a connecting link between chapter 1 and chapters 3—4?

   _____

   _____

   _____

   _____

2. Read Jonah 3 and answer the following questions.

   a. Describe the Lord's message that came to Jonah a second time.

   _____

   _____

   _____

Jonah 2 — Praise God, He Delivers from Death

b. State specifically what message Jonah preached.

_____

_____

_____

_____

_____

_____

c. Describe how the people of Nineveh responded to Jonah's preaching.

_____

_____

_____

d. Describe the people of Nineveh in the country of Assyria. If you have access to a Bible dictionary, consult it.

_____

_____

_____

_____

_____

LESSON TWELVE

e. How did God react to Nineveh's response to the message?

_____

_____

_____

_____

_____

3. Read Jonah 4 and answer the following questions.

a. How did Jonah feel about God's response Nineveh's repentance? Why?

_____

_____

_____

_____

_____

b. What did Jonah know about God that caused him to disobey God's original call (see 4:1)?

_____

_____

_____

_____

_____

JONAH 2 —PRAISE GOD, HE DELIVERS FROM DEATH   319

    c. How is God's compassion contrasted to Jonah's attitude (see 4:9-11)?

_____

_____

_____

_____

_____

_____

Summary. Briefly summarize your observations below.

My Findings

1. What kind of Christian does Jonah represent?

_____

_____

_____

_____

2. What does the book of Jonah reveal about God?

_____

_____

_____

_____

3. Record any other discoveries you made in the book of Jonah.

___

DISCERN

Now that you have examined the contextual setting of the book of Jonah, you are ready to consider the message of Jonah's thanksgiving song. Jonah 2:1 looks back to chapter 1. Jonah 2:10 looks forward to chapters 3 – 4. Therefore, verses 2-9 will be your focus in the Discern section. Your overview of the entire book has created a framework for interpreting Jonah's psalm.

Jonah 2 —Praise God, He Delivers from Death

Pause for Prayer

You have commanded us To keep Your precepts diligently. Oh, that my ways were directed To keep Your statutes! Then I would not be ashamed, When I look into all Your commandments. I will praise You with uprightness of heart, When I learn Your righteous judgments (Psalm 119:4-7).

You have already discovered that Jonah knew about God's grace, compassion, lovingkindness, and willingness to cancel judgment against people. Jonah's thanksgiving psalm celebrates those characteristics of God. As you pray, ask the Holy Spirit to help you remember instances in your own life that testified to those same truths. Strive to strengthen your own faith in God's character. It will be a confidence that not only secures your relationship with God, but also enables you to counsel others that God is willing to forgive all sins, even our own willing disobedience.

Key Words Open the Door to Understanding

Read Jonah's thanksgiving psalm several times, looking for repeated words and phrases, and record them below. List key words and divine names below, and on your key word list and mark them in the text. Be sure to transfer common key words from your past lists. Give attention to the pronouns in the song, linking them to God, Jonah, or others.

_____

_____

_____

322   Lesson Twelve

_____
_____
_____
_____

1. What is the most common divine name used in chapter 2? How many times is it used?

   _____
   _____
   _____

2. Jonah's name occurs only two times in chapter 2. More often, Jonah is referred to by what pronouns? How many times?

   _____
   _____
   _____

3. God is referred to many times with pronouns. List the pronouns used. Include the number of times God is referred to by a pronoun.

   _____
   _____
   _____

4. With each lesson in this study, you have added to your knowledge of God's character. In Lesson Eleven, you discovered God as *Elohim*, or *Creator*. As Creator, God is sovereign over all of His

creation. Jonah's song proclaims the same truth in descriptive language. List Jonah's expressions that reveal God's control over creation.

Verse	Revelation of God's Sovereignty Over Creation
3	
3	
6	
10	

5. Continuing in this vein, write below any words or phrases that reveal God's character. Then transfer each reference to the margin of your Bible.

Verse	God's Character

Lesson Twelve

Key Insights About the Text

1. Notice how Jonah expresses his relationship to God. Record the phrases below.

v. 1	
v. 2	

2. The psalm moves from problem to resolution. Record the problem and the resolution below.

v. 1 Problem	
v. 10 Resolution	

3. *Sheol* (v.2) is the region of the dead, an aggressive force that comes after a person in trouble, trying to extinguish their life. The word is used figuratively in this song. Jonah also uses poetic verse to describe his plight in the second phrase of verse 6. Write the phrase below and explain how you interpret its meaning.

_____
_____
_____
_____
_____

Why do you think Jonah sang of death in his song?

_____
_____
_____
_____
_____

4. The word *soul* occurs twice in this song (vv. 5, 7). In the Hebrew culture, *soul* represented the very essence of life. This is why the Great Commandment calls on us to love the Lord God with all our soul (Deut. 6:5). When the soul is in jeopardy, life itself is at risk. Knowing this, rewrite these two verses to explain Jonah's meaning in contemporary language.

v. 5	
v. 7	

Lesson Twelve

5. Verse 8 seems to intrude into the song. Let's take a closer look at the historical context to better understand its meaning. Jonah was a prophet in the northern kingdom of Israel (2 Kings 14:25) during the reign of Jeroboam II. The song presupposes that we understand that many Israelites in Jonah's time period worshipped idols. Read verses 8 and 9 and notice Jonah's contrast between idol worship and his own worship. Keep in mind that words such as nevertheless, but, and however often indicate contrast.

Verse	Contrasting Word	Contrasting Phrases
v. 8		
v. 9		

What does this contrast tell you about Jonah's heart when he was at death's door?
_____
_____
_____
_____
_____

JONAH 2 — PRAISE GOD, HE DELIVERS FROM DEATH

_____
_____
_____
_____
_____

6. Draw a box around verse 9 in the text, which is the key verse for Jonah 2.

7. The essential structure of the thanksgiving psalm is present in Jonah's song. Identify the reference for each element below.

Element	Verse Locations
Intent to Praise	
Report of Deliverance	
Renewed Vow of Praise	

My Observations

8. Tell what God does to Jonah according to the song. Note the verse reference next to each observation.

_____
_____
_____

LESSON TWELVE

_____
_____
_____
_____
_____
_____
_____

9. Describe Jonah's actions according to the song. Again, note the verse reference next to each observation.

_____
_____
_____
_____
_____
_____

10. List other observations that you have made about Jonah's song.

_____
_____
_____
_____
_____
_____

My Interpretation

You have seen how the thanksgiving psalms were birthed in particular historical situations. Many of those psalms were added to the Book of Psalms during its development over many centuries. Summarize what you have learned from this embedded psalm below.

DEVOTE

Jonah 2 reflects a personal crisis between God and a disobedient prophet. It also witnesses to the character of God as One who is gracious, compassionate, and full of lovingkindness. In the midst of crisis, Jonah repents and God forgives. He is truly a God of second chances. As you come to this important milestone in studying Jonah 2, let the Holy Spirit speak to you about what God's forgiveness means in your life—past, present, and future.

Think about people you know who struggle with accepting God's forgiveness. Some people find it difficult to believe that God can, or will, forgive *all* sins. Sins such as child abuse, rape, and abortion have long-term effects on both perpetrators and victims. Other sins include consequences that cannot be reversed (e.g., murder). Yet God is willing to forgive *all* sins—yours and everyone else's. Allow the Holy Spirit to plant this truth deep in your spirit. It will give you confidence to approach God in your failures. It will enable you to remind others with assurance that God will forgive *all* their sins.

Pause for Prayer

My hands also I will lift up to Your commandments, Which I love, And I will meditate on Your statutes (Psalm 119:48).

A time-proven way to hear from God about the applied meaning of a biblical text is called *lectio divina*, a *spiritual* reading of the biblical text. *Lectio divina* is one of the spiritual disciplines that has been used for centuries as a structured way to engage with God. This prayer experience has four components: reading, meditating, praying, and contemplating.

First, read the Scripture slowly and meditate on what the text means for you. Second, read the text again as you prayerfully listen for God's message to you. Finally, read the text a third time and open your heart to what God wants you to *do* in response to His Word. Take time right now to practice this discipline.

Step 1: Read Jonah 2:1-10 slowly, reflecting on what the Spirit is saying to you through this text. Write what you sense the Spirit saying.

_____
_____
_____
_____
_____

Lesson Twelve

___

Step 2: Read Jonah 2:1-10 a second time, listening for the voice of the Spirit.

Write what you sense the Spirit saying.

___

Step 3: Slowly read Jonah 2:1-10 a third time.

This is the Word of God. What do you sense the Holy Spirit saying about the truths in the text as they apply to your life?

___

JONAH 2 —PRAISE GOD, HE DELIVERS FROM DEATH

_____
_____
_____
_____
_____
_____
_____

DISCIPLE

The final and ultimate step in Bible study is to *act* on what you have learned. Knowing God's Word is never enough. We must actualize it in our lives. The parable of the Good Samaritan (Luke 10:25-37) illustrates that those who know God's Word do not necessarily put it into action. Consider the actions of the priest and Levite in the story. The Levite had proven that he knew God's law when he spoke it to Jesus. Though he knew God's will, he refused to help the wounded stranger. Ezra provides a much better example of what God wants from His people. Ezra "prepared his heart to seek the Law of the Lord, and to do it, and to teach statutes and ordinances in Israel" (Ezra 7:10).

As you review your prayerful experience with the lectio divina, think about what God would have you do. Write down your thoughts.

Commit to obey Him in the coming weeks. If it is not too personal, share your commitment with a close Christian friend, increasing the possibility that you will do it. But more than anything, obey God out of your gratitude.

Thanks Be Unto God, His Mercy Endures Forever

We pray that your study of the thanksgiving psalms has illuminated *A Pathway to Praise*. Praise is the rightful response to God for all His blessings and faithfulness. We often think about divine deliverance only in terms of rescue from evil or tragedy. God's deliverance in those situations is most evident, and gratitude springs up naturally. Yet the Lord's deliverance sometimes comes in the form of blessings. Our wellbeing results from God's providential care and protection. Job understood this reality. In the midst of his affliction, he reflected back on an earlier time in his life when all was well.

> *² "Oh, that I were as in months past, As in the days when God watched over me; ³ When His lamp shone upon my head, And when by His light I walked through darkness; ⁴ Just as I was in the days of my prime, When the friendly counsel of God was over my tent; ⁵ When the Almighty was yet with me, When my children were around me; ⁶ When my steps were bathed with cream, And the rock poured out rivers of oil for me!* (Job 29:2-6)

In good times and bad times, we should live in thanksgiving and praise. The thanksgiving psalms celebrate God's deliverance, both visible and invisible. Let their words become part of your lifestyle of praise.

About the Author

Jerome Boone teaches in two key areas of the School of Religion at Lee University: Christian Formation and Biblical Studies. In Christian Formation, he explores issues related to how people come to faith, how Christians mature in the faith, and why some lose their faith. He also practices and teaches the classical Christian disciplines (e.g., prayer, Bible reading) as pathways to spiritual development and renewal. In Biblical Studies, he teaches survey courses for both the Old and New Testaments as well as courses on the prophets, Psalms, and wisdom literature. He strives to engage in the constructive work of relating the scriptures to our everyday lives. Dr. Boone's current research is in the area of biblical and theological foundations of worship, as well as hermeneutics. He presents regularly at conferences of the Society for Pentecostal Studies.

Sandra (Sandi) served in the corporate world as administrative assistant, in the academic world as tutorial coordinator, and in the community of faith as a leader in women's ministries and teacher of inductive Bible studies. Her role in writing this study with Jerome has been a special delight. She has worn many hats, but the one she cherishes most is that of facilitator of life dreams for her husband,

Jerome; her daughter and son-in-law, Darla and Bill Gallentine, both pediatricians in North Carolina; her son and daughter-in-law, David, an internal medicine physician, and Danielle, a school teacher in Virginia; and her grandchildren, Caleb and Gabe Gallentine, and Tanner and Grace Boone.